All rights reserved. No part of this publication may be reproduced, stored in a retrieval system or transmitted in any form or by any means, electronic, mechanical, photocopying, recording or otherwise, without the written permission of the author.

Text copyright © 2018 Jay LaRico

Content Editing by Betty Hoeffner and Charlie Cochran

Front and Back Cover design by Betty Hoeffner and Al Baker

Library of Congress Control Number: 2018909146

ISBN-13: 978-0-9759004-3-7
Printed in the United States of America

To buy additional copies of this book email TheChoiceOfAngels@gmail.com
Quantity discounts are available for bulk purchases

The Choice Of Angels

An Alzheimer's Caregiver's 11 Year Journey

By Jay LaRico

Dedicated to my mother

Mary Betty LaRico

The Karma of T-Bones and Bit-a-Honey®
has come full circle

Contents

Dedication 4
Forward 6
Our End, Your Beginning 9
Introduction 10
Making The Decision. 12
No, It's Not Like Raising Children. 16
The Grind 19
Beware The Dark Side 21
S.O.S. 24
Finding Las Vegas 27
Ya Gotta Have Faith 30
Home Is Where The Heart Is 33
That's Entertainment 36
The Grand Illusion 38
Never Say Never 41
Peek - A - Boo 43
Opportunity Detoured 46
Unregrettable 48
Zippers And Buttons And Strings, Oh My! 51
Reasons 53
A Funny Thing Happened On The Way Home From The Hospital 63
A Day In The Life 67
Reversal Of Misfortune 76
P.S. I LOVE YOU 80
The End 82
Before And After Pictures of My Mom and Notes She Wrote 86
About The Author 88
Grazie Mille 89
Book Signing/Speaker Contact Information 90

FORWARD
By
DR. JOSEPH H. FLAHERTY

This delicate but honest account not only exposes the true nature of being a caregiver for someone with Alzheimer's disease, but it raises the job of caregiving to a level of respect near motherhood. This is not to be confused with the misconception that caring for an older person with this disease is similar to caring for a child, as the author so eloquently explains. It is to say that these caregivers are the silent saints of today, the hidden hope of the burning question, "What is our society going to do with the growing number of people with Alzheimer's disease?" Jay LaRico provides us with one of the best answers we have available.

Alzheimer's is one of the most devastating diseases I have ever had to deal with. To care for a person with Alzheimer's disease is frustrating, emotionally upsetting and physically wearisome. And this is what it feels like for me, a doctor, someone who only has to care for the person with Alzheimer's disease once in a while in a clinic, or in a hospital. I can distance myself from the problems once I leave the room. Can you imagine what it would be like if you were not able to leave the room?

Well, now you can. Through the eyes, ears emotions and every other sense that is involved in being a caregiver for someone with Alzheimer's disease, you can begin to understand, in what Jay LaRico writes, is "The path that becomes an adventure of unrestricted possibilities and simple moments that move the heart and make the pain worthwhile."

I would add to his intentions for writing this book, that of helping people who are already caregivers or are contemplating becoming caregivers, that this book can also help any health care professional who might even come across only one patient with Alzheimer's disease, any politician who has to consider the health and well being of all citizens and any friend or relative of a person who is a caregiver. In other words, since Alzheimer's disease touches every part of our society, especially through the caregiver, for any person who lives in our society today, this book is a must read.

Alzheimer's disease is reported to be the 4th leading cause of death due to disease in people over 65 in the U.S. It is estimated that annual treatment costs approach $100 billion annually. The prevalence of this disease is still increasing and with the aging of the US population, the number of individuals with Alzheimer's disease is expected to quadruple over the next 50 years.

But every disease has big numbers. Although the often misleading percent of "elderly" (defined as those over 65) who have Alzheimer's, turns out to be only 5%, a more realistic question may be, what are your chances of getting this disease, or "worse" yet, your chances of becoming a caregiver? Do you really have only a 1 in 20 chance of getting this disease? The answer is no, because this 5% is based on everyone over age 65 at one point in time, that is, the current total population in this age group. If we look at the percentage of people over age 65 during the rest of their life, it turns out that more than 33% of women and 20% of men aged 65 and older will develop some type of dementia of which Alzheimer's is the most common type. That is a 1 in 3 to 1 in 5 chance of getting this dreaded disease. If you add to this your chance of becoming a caregiver, these numbers could essentially double. And despite the hope for a cure, not only is a cure many years away, a "pure" cure where the disease will be completely reversed is unlikely. So we, as a society, will likely always have people with Alzheimer's disease, and thus we will always be caregivers.

The good news that Jay LaRico is trying to share with us is that although being a caregiver is hard, even painful, it is the thing to do. The negatives, although mountainous, are eventually outweighed by the positives. In his chapter, "Never Say Never," one can begin to understand how it is possible for caregivers to do the unthinkable, because, "you begin to see the profound impact that your sacrifice is having, if only for brief moments." He gives hope to tired caregivers in his chapter, "The Grind" as he explains why it "is just part of the deal. It is probably the most integral aspect of the caregiving process, because it keeps the familiar close and this seems to ease the disposition of our loved one." Jay LaRico also tells us through his many real and sometimes daunting experiences, not only how to deal with the "Dark Side" of this disease and how to take necessary respite times form caregiving, but also how to understand and even love the one who is causing unthinkable stress.

Finally, it must be said, that the first time one reads Jay LaRico's story, thoughts such as "I don't believe it could be that bad," or "ooh that is so crude," are likely to surface. But that is the beauty of this book. It is real, it is true and Jay LaRico does not hold back. It is the second time when one reads this book that one starts to truly appreciate the saintliness of caregiving for someone with Alzheimer's disease, And although Jay LaRico would deny he could possibly be on anyone's list for sainthood, he is at least an accidental hero who discovers how to survive and sometimes find joy on this unimaginable journey. The consequence of his actions, and actions of every other caregiver in this situation, is the ultimate reward of caregiving: compassion. In The Choice of Angels, Jay LaRico shows us how to truly "be with" our loved one with Alzheimer's, despite time and the disease itself taking them away from us.

OUR END, YOUR BEGINNING

It was a cold, snowing April morning when Mom had finally had enough of the silly, seesaw that is St. Louis weather. Her labored breathing was silent now. No more valiant attempts to persevere; instead, she ignored Dylan Thomas and went gently. At approximately nine o'clock that glooming Monday morning, Mary Betty LaRico finally let go.

I sat there in a loud silence, holding her hand and experiencing a time warp of sorts that will haunt me for the rest of my life. Although I gave a Herculean effort on her behalf, at that moment I couldn't shake the feeling I had done something wrong. The, *if I'd only* game was playing on a loop in my head, fueling tears and fears and obscuring an already obscure situation. However, as I began to make the phone calls and arrangements, caring for Mom one final time, I knew that game was merely a facade. In reality...I did everything right.

From making the commitment to care for my mother, through 11-years of riding along on the rollercoaster that is Alzheimer's disease, my time with her was spot on. The following explores that rollercoaster ride and hopefully helps others who are standing in line preparing for the emotional thrill of a lifetime.

INTRODUCTION

She called me a son of a bitch and followed up that flattering bit of encouragement by uttering her favorite axiom...shit ass! But, I suppose that adage was appropriate since I was helping her wipe, following the bedtime bathroom visit. Early on she would get extremely irritated with my assistance in the bathroom but would forget it all before she hit the sheets. You see, my mother had Alzheimer's disease and I took on the caregiver roll in an attempt to braid her final threads of reality together in order to keep her spirit in our house...not the home.

For 11-years I was the sole caregiver for my mother. Hopefully, the following pages will help others who find themselves in my situation smile, laugh and cope. They will provide a realistic view of what seems to be an imponderable situation, not only for the caregiver but every family member and friend affected by this dilemma. The words will shed light on the predicament of the caregiver for those contemplating the challenge or for those who know someone who has taken on the caregiver role. Most importantly, I hope my words will show everyone that Alzheimer's, or any debilitating illness, is not the end of the journey. Instead, it is merely a fork in the path of one final trek; a pilgrimage that becomes an adventure of unrestricted possibilities and simple moments which move the heart and make the pain worthwhile.

As I began writing this book I felt it was time to share my experiences. People were constantly asking me how I do what I do. How do I deal with the reality of putting the prime years of my life on hold in order to care for someone who really can't appreciate the sacrifice? They were curious about the terrain of the high road when it is traversed alone. Mostly, they were of the opinion I had landed in a sort of purgatory and questioned the quandary I have chosen to confront. Those observations, and many more, were instrumental in prompting me to share my experience.

In a nut shell, I wanted to share it all; not just the happy times but the frightening times, too. Those moments when hell seemed to be knocking on the door and St. Peter was on the verge of pulling my file. I want everyone to know those times are part of the deal. I want the reader to understand how to handle those moments and know those times are well worth it.

MAKING THE DECISION

There are many decisions that have to be made when dealing with Alzheimer's, but the most important, by far, is the resolution to become a full time caregiver. The quality and comfort with which your loved one lives out their remaining days of awareness rests solely on your decision. The old adage, "If I'd only known then, what I know now," is a constant throughout the caregiving process. Unknown diversions around virtually every turn test your resolve and exemplify that statement. The truth is, for me, I'd still do it. However, if this is your *then*, I'm going to give you some of the flavor of *now*, so you can swirl it around and see how it tastes.

After it became clear that Alzheimer's had indeed dug its claws into the mind of my mother, the buzz among the siblings was, "what are we going to do with her?" Suddenly, she went from the woman who was integral in molding our lives, to a burden referred to as *her*, that we had to do something with. It was true some decisions had to be made and something did have to be done, but compassion and contemplation needed to be a big part of the equation and they weren't. Perhaps it would help if I explained the geography and fellowship of our situation in order to help define this dilemma and the consequent decision that was made.

My mother, widowed in 1976, lived in St. Louis, where our entire family got its start. My older brother is a small business owner in St. Louis and my younger brother is married and is a salesman and musician there as well. My older sister lives in Indiana and runs Hey U.G.L.Y. - Unique Gifted Lovable You, a nonprofit organization that is saving the lives of youth who are suicidal because of being bullied-www.HeyUGLY.org. My younger sister is married, the mother of two and lives in Dallas with her family. And me, as you've surmised, am the middle kid who, at the time, was living in Kansas City, MO and self-employed as a free-lance writer, building contractor and property manager.

So there we were, five different siblings living five different and hectic lives, looking at a mother who was soon going to need a lot more attention than she had required in the past. That's when the phone calls began. It was posturing more than anything else, mostly by the older two. The oldest, my brother, was strongly against putting mom in a nursing home. His concern at the time was money, which in and of itself is a large part of the decision making process. However, this decision should never interfere with the well-being of the owner of the money. Having said that, his concern was money, wrapped neatly in a cloak of spiritual, homeopathic mumbo jumbo. My younger sister struggled with the situation and contemplated taking mom in, but being a mother herself, with two young children at the time, that option wouldn't have been fair to anyone. She and my younger brother went the nursing home route, devising a fairytale full of happy hours, eligible bachelors and 24 hour a day ice cream to sell their concept. My younger brother even went as far as to put down a deposit at a high-end area nursing home, barking, "Only the best for my mom!" As a side note, the two younger siblings were all but invisible during my 11-years with mom. In any event, this illusion was just the ticket necessary to sell my older sister. The nursing home became a means to an end, with no real regard for my mother.

Before I go any further, it seems important to point out the obvious; no two families have the same history or dynamic. In many respects my family wasn't as close as most families. But then again, we were closer than a lot of families. I've noticed, through observations and conversations, that the stronger the family core, the more support the caregiver receives. If you're considering taking on caregiving responsibilities, look within the circle of your family and evaluate its strength and thusly the caliber of support you will receive. This was one aspect I overlooked when making my decision and one I would have mentally prepared for.

With the decision all but written in stone, I found myself sitting in Kansas City, trying to process the verdict which had come down from the others. Ever since the Alzheimer's diagnosis, I began making more trips to St. Louis and tried to call mom at least once a day. With this, I had a comfortable gauge on her abilities, as well as the obvious declines. I knew the days of her living safely on her own were numbered, but the thought of placing her in a nursing home, regardless of how posh, just wasn't sitting well with me. This is a woman, who in her later years had finally found her voice. She was traveling and dating and enjoying a life the mother of five seldom gets to discover. After so many years of living within the boundaries life had appointed her, destiny had finally set her free...then irony stepped in. These thoughts and a nagging sense of anxiousness caused my first contemplations of caregiving and prompted more phone calls and many sleepless nights.

I'm the kind of guy who needs to throw ideas off of family and friends so I might get the affirmation to do what I already know is right. I called friends first; mostly people who knew me well but had no connection to my family. They all said the same thing and had the same concerns; you've got to take care of your mom, and, how will you make a living? Even the people I knew didn't want me to leave Kansas City encouraged me to do so. Their token sacrifices went a long way in helping with my decision. Eventually, I phoned my older brother to share my contemplations of caregiving, holding him to strict confidence so as not to get pressured into a decision I wasn't yet sure of. As you can imagine, he was elated at the possibility of my solution and was extremely supportive. He reminded me of a politician making glossy promises to a would-be contributor or voter, and this made me nervous. Nevertheless, I was leaning heavily towards the caregiving commitment and decided to get the opinion of the one person everyone had left out of this debate...my mother.

The conversation with mom was the deal breaker and one I'll never forget. You know, as I think about it, it's hard to imagine that sort of coherent conversation coming from my mother. In any event, we talked about nothing for a few minutes, "What did you have for breakfast? How's the weather," etc. Eventually I steered the conversation towards Alzheimer's and could feel the tension rattle through the phone. According to her, the whole world was crazy, including "That doctor," and she just wished everyone would leave her alone. I explained to her that being alone wasn't going to be an option much longer and then relayed the opinion of the majority. The reticence which followed was deafening. I now understood what Simon and Garfunkel were talking about. Her trembling voice broke the silence with a simple plea..."I grew up in a home; please don't let me die in one." The Masons raised my mother, along with her three younger brothers. Her father had died when she was very young and the economy of the times was not conducive for Grandmother to raise four children. Luckily, my Grandfather was a Mason and the Masonic home was mom's home until her teen years. You can understand why the thought of another term of confinement would concern her.

It's hard for me to say no in general, but with this plea lying on the table, it was impossible. So there I was and that is how I got there. It's not going to be the same for everyone, and maybe not anyone, but the fact remains hard decisions have got to be made when dealing with Alzheimer's. But, they have to be made with love and a full understanding of what terrain your commitment will cover. Hopefully my words will give an accurate glimpse of the map required to traverse this real estate.

NO, IT'S NOT LIKE RAISING CHILDREN

Some people are of the opinion caring for a loved one with Alzheimer's is just like raising children. My younger sister, far removed from the realities of Alzheimer's was always, *welcoming me to her world*, forming some quasi-parallel between her motherhood experiences and the stories I shared with her. Nothing could be further from the truth. Although in many ways Alzheimer's victims are very childlike, they are without a doubt, not children. In most cases they are our parents, which make the comparison slippery at best.

How could these comparisons even be made? Well, if you are new at this, or considering caregiving in the future, the answer to that question can best be given through example. The illustrations in this book are not intended to discourage, they are merely moments of madness, a few of the many marvelous moments that will grace the path of your adventure.

There was a time when using toilet paper was a step often overlooked by my mother. She would go through the normal motions but forgot the toilet paper part. Yuck! Now, if my mother was just like a child, playing with her poopy might seem cute. If she were a child, you could explain the concept of toilet paper, you could stress the germ factor and you could tell her, "Big girls never use their hands and always use toilet paper." In time this technique would be successful...if she were a child. On the other hand (no pun intended), since my mother had schooled five children in the fine art of the toilet and, since she does in fact have Alzheimer's disease, the skill of learning is not an option. The reality of the situation is as far to the other side of the spectrum from cute as you can get. There are no special techniques to get you through this dilemma. No Doctor Spock type manuals to turn to for guidance. You must simply be patient, understanding and attentive while waiting for this odd phase to pass. I found if I put mom on a bathroom schedule of every two hours, I could control the paper situation and insure a cleaner circumstance. I simply stood outside the door and when it was determined she'd finished, I provided paper and a little assistance in order to help complete the task. On a similar note, as the Alzheimer's progressed, mom was storing a tremendous amount of urine, simply forgetting the urge was there. The bathroom schedule was beneficial in that area as well. This routine is essential, not only for paper management but for health reasons as well. Allowing urine to sit, unrelieved, is the main ingredient for bladder infections and unsanitary wiping habits can fertilize a number of conditions.

Another unusual situation dealt with the *destruction and mutilation* of almost anything my mother could get her hands on. Of all of the interesting traits I saw with this disease, this, according to the other caregivers and experts I had talked with, is the most common. It is something you really must prepare for as I will discuss it in greater detail in another chapter. In any event, if a child were to display this sort of behavior you could scold, punish or simply remove the items and slowly re-introduce them as the lesson was learned. In many ways, this behavior is a rite of passage for children. With Alzheimer's you can only eliminate and monitor. In my case, I finally had to remove all of my mother's clothes and store them in the guest bedroom. Eventually I removed everything but her bed and a lamp in order to save my sanity. Still, from time to time, she would manage to sneak in a tissue or a page from some unsuspecting magazine and rip it to her heart's content.

I could go on and on but you get the small part of the argument...Alzheimer's victims have lost the ability to learn. Children can, and usually do. However, the strongest part of this debate is that these people are, in most cases, the elders of our world, parents who taught us the basic skills of life we take for granted on a daily basis. Our protectors, who now can't wipe or reason or recognize, even their own children. People, who due to the luck of the draw, or maybe the introduction of aluminum or aluminum-byproducts into their young lives, are now paying the ultimate price...their memories. These rocks we once leaned on for everything are crumbling before our eyes and we didn't even get a chance to say goodbye. Just like raising children? I can only wish.

THE GRIND

A situation we *doers of good deeds* never really consider, but one that will continue to creep into our reality, is the simple grind of day-to-day life. We all have our routines; our idiosyncratic rituals that somehow help make each day our own. But when the mundane necessities of our loved one begin to infiltrate our personal program, tension tends to sprout in our subconscious, As a caregiver, you will find personal space is an endangered luxury floating on the same list with the bald eagle and the giant Panda. So, when simple routines we rely on to manage our day-to-day life are obstructed, the weight becomes oppressive and the need to recognize and adapt is paramount. I usually began my day, as many of us do, with that most beloved cup of coffee. In the real world I would sip that hot cup of diligence and plan the upcoming day. It was a groove I was comfortable with and one, when disrupted, seemed to affect every other aspect of my day. Can you say addictive? I still followed that ritual during my time with mom; however, instead of planning the day, I used the time to prepare my psyche for the new rut I had chosen to follow.

Most mornings I didn't get a chance to shower, save the spray that would hit me while assisting mom. For me, the shower was an integral part of the morning ritual I spoke of. Not only was it a cleanliness issue, it was also the perfect distraction while waiting for my coffee to brew. As a caregiver, shower time was rare, but on the upside, I did savor those showers so much more.

The grind, as I call it, is the schedule of things that must be done for your loved one, day in and day out. These are usually the simple undertakings they can no longer perform alone. For example: I began each day waking my mother, coaxing her from bed to bathroom, getting her into and out of the shower, helping her dry off, making sure she brushed her teeth, guiding her through the dressing process and then helping her downstairs to begin her day. Once there, we struggled with shoes and sox, brushed her hair and this is when the weight of the grind always seemed to slap me. Voices from unknown tongues began to ask questions I just didn't want to hear. Logic began to steer the dialect down paths I know are treacherous, yet I would hesitate at that crossroads every day. Finally, hair in place and looking as cute as ever, I sat mom on the sofa, popped in a Shirley Temple DVD and that usually stole her attention long enough for me to prepare breakfast.

Breakfast was usually my first opportunity to stand back and appreciate the worth of my decision. Early on there was always a moment when mom would become very animated and utter a very sincere, "delicious." I knew it wasn't necessarily my unique culinary skills she was commenting on but she was acknowledging taste and possibly me, and at that moment, the grind would begin to ease up a bit. Of course, breakfast soon came to an end, and, as the lines continued to connect the same dots on the same picture, we would go on, traveling down the frightfully familiar path, seeking miraculous moments to maintain our momentum and bear the weight of the grind.

You see, the grind is just part of the deal. It is probably the most integral aspect of the caregiving process, because it keeps the familiar close and this seems to ease the disposition of our loved ones. And remember, at the end of the day, you have to ask yourself one question: "Is the quality of life you are providing for your loved one superior to that of a nursing home?" As long as you can answer yes, as I could, then nothing else matters and the grind, as well as any other obstacle, is well worth grappling with.

BEWARE THE DARK SIDE
(But acknowledge its existence)

Mother Theresa and Gandhi aside, there will be times when this disease is just too much to handle. A surrealistic cloud will hover, raining down thoughts of malicious lethargy. "Nobody can be this stupid," thunders sarcastically from the heavens. Instead of acknowledging why this is happening, you will ask, "Why are *they* doing this?" Of course, you know why this is happening, you've known since the day you embarked on this adventure. Still, you find yourself, from time-to-time, grappling with the enormous absurdity of this reality. And it's not as if you're harboring some clinical denial about this disease. You are more than aware of the what's and why's of Alzheimer's. However, the logical you will find the symptoms inane and just too uncharacteristic for your loved one. This is when the dark side enters your psyche. Pseudo paranoia breeches the peace you have worked so hard to achieve. It's insane...confusion is amplified and multiplied and the dark side is laying in wait, prepared to pounce on your wounded resilience.

And even when you think you have the dark side held at bay, it somehow finds its way into your head, nudging your patience in an attempt to disrupt tranquility. Its cunning voice whispers parental commands and ultimatums as a means to tame the lunacy you see in your loved one. But, you must resist, for these tactics require a learned response in order to circumvent any given issue. The dark side will use this ploy, knowing full well learning is not an option here. It will stir frustration in hopes of conquering your spirit. On numerous occasions I fell prey to this ruse, attempting to employ child psychology in hopes of curbing non-mom like behavior.

Occasionally, when your defense is strong, the dark side will creep into your unsuspecting loved one, setting off a flurry of Linda Blair inspired moments in hopes of breaking you down. An unfamiliar appearance will shroud their already altered face and rage will fill once tranquil eyes. At this point you must harness all of your strength, liberate your love, and stand firmly with your faith in order to deflect this barrage of baffling belligerence. This is the most difficult aspect of caregiving. Anger seems to manifest itself as randomly as the reels stop on a slot machine. Unfortunately, the possibility of a jackpot never exists with these episodes. Instead, there are aggravation, agitation and adolescent accusations. Words reserved for the gutter flow fundamentally from a mouth, save the dark side, that could never conceive such obscenity.

In my case, this angry, potty mouth was my mother. Through observation, and with plenty of examples to dissect, I have formed my own hypothesis as to the cause of these tirades. I noticed each time there was an outburst, it was centered on some simple correction or otherwise normal routine of life she just couldn't quite grasp. I believe somewhere deep within her mind, there is a slender section of consciousness drifting aimlessly, dodging the disease and occasionally recognizing perplexing situations. This is when the primal instincts kick in and all hell breaks loose. It's like when we were kids and the other children made fun of that extra short haircut or the paisley shirt our mothers made us wear on the first day of school. There were two options to take...ignore the ridicule or fight back. I think the fighting back is what happens when our loved one has a foggy notion 'something is rotten on Denmark.' I have no idea what that statement means, exactly, but a teacher of mine used it frequently and it seems to fit here. The point is, she knew she should know how to wipe, or chew, or put her shoes on the right feet. And, in that moment when she realized she did it wrong, she suddenly had on that paisley shirt and she would fight back.

You must constantly be on the lookout for this dilemma for it is always there; however, recognition is only half the battle. Find a way to deflect the dark powers it employs in order to maintain peace. If anger and confusion begin to sway to either side, take a quick time out. A nap for your loved one is a great remedy. Talk of rest and sweet dreams usually does the trick and the separation you desperately need is achieved. It is not lazy or cowardice to take this route...it is essential! Peace and harmony are paramount to the caregiving experience. Do not be afraid to do whatever it takes to keep tranquility in your environment. Love is a great motivator and I assume you wouldn't be reading this if love wasn't a big part of your equation. However, when dealing with Alzheimer's, love needs to make way for reason and common sense. With time, this tactic will wear down the powers of the dark side and peace will help fuel the love that is already abundant in your home.

S.O.S.

As your caregiving responsibilities begin to mount and the pressure of the day-to-day "grind" begins dragging down your disposition, the time to seek outside help is at hand. As I began this journey I vowed to never accept outside assistance that wasn't family. Why had I made this sacrifice if only to hand off my responsibilities to a stranger? Well, that's when I was wearing the shoes that now warm your feet. As time passed, I realized, in order to take care of my mother properly, I had to take care of myself first.

There will come a time when the need for some temporary relief is essential. If there aren't family members available to give you that timely break, you must seek outside assistance in order to maintain the strength and discipline required to fulfill your task. There are many avenues to travel, and many obstacles to avoid when seeking the support you require. Be prudent, there are far too many choices and too many people who are only in it for the money, not the welfare of your loved one. It seems taking care of old, confused human beings has become very profitable and the lure of easy money brings out the darkest of entrepreneurs.

When the time came for me, mother and I scoured the area, investigating many examples of adult daycare and short term respite facilities. Some situations weren't equipped to handle Alzheimer's and they were forthcoming and, many times, helpful in aiding our quest. A few of the facilities required my mother be able to respond to a fire alarm, something I hadn't even thought of at the time. Of course, that wasn't an option so the expedition continued. What we were going to need was a *lock down* unit. This is simply a section of a nursing home that has no exit access without a key code or some other means of security. It is widely known that Alzheimer's victims have a tendency to roam. Personally, I never had to deal with that dilemma but we hear too often of people with Alzheimer's who have gone missing after wandering from their homes. Early on I wasn't too comfortable with this option because most units held many later stage patients and it was hard seeing my mother among them. However, the facility I finally settled on was outstanding at separating apples from oranges; keeping the early stage patients occupied with various activities while still paying close attention to the more severe. Not only did they provide me with worry-free assistance, they also provided a crystal ball of sorts with which I was able to see the future and begin to mentally prepare for what I would be in for.

Efficiency and professionalism aside, the key factor in making the decision on a respite facility, or adult daycare center, had nothing to do with ambiance. We had visited many very luxurious locations that were professional and accommodating in almost every way. The one thing I noticed is they all directed their attention to me. After all, I did have the check book. Finally, we walked into what would be our last stop in the hunt for a respite facility. It wasn't elegant, it didn't have a sentry or a grand lobby with which to woo. However, we were greeted immediately and, after introductions were made, the strangest thing happened...the representative we were speaking with gently took my mother's hand, placed and arm around her shoulder, asking is she might like to stay with them a few days. During the entire scope of our search, not one person directed any welcome of personal attention to my mother. I hadn't really thought about it until I saw the immediate connection made at this final facility. My heart warmed, my anxiety lowered and I knew my quest for a respite facility was complete.

The search for an adult daycare facility was a journey through a depressing black hole filled with folding chairs and overcrowded spaces. It was a disillusioning trip with no hope of success on the horizon. Then serendipity stepped in. My mother had a friend, an angel really, who began to take mom for a few hours every Wednesday after she recognized the toll the apparent apathy of my family was taking on me. That friend was participating in some charitable activity at a local hospital and her husband and I took mom to the event to support the cause. While there, a representative of the hospital got wind of my story and recommended the adult daycare facility they had on the premises. Once again hugs and conversation directed at my mother were abundant during the interview and that center became an answer to a prayer for me.

The point of it all is simple...you just can't do it alone! If you find yourself in a similar situation, seek help. Just remember to be thorough, patient and always keep an eye out for a hug. It might be an old saying, but it bears repeating here, "You can't take care of someone else if you don't take care of yourself, first."

FINDING LAS VEGAS

As mom and I began our journey, there were many things that concerned me, even though I was definitely all in with my commitment. Money, privacy and me time were at the top of the list...stress, however was never a consideration. Nothing I had read or heard lead me to consider that most prominent aspect of my decision. I knew it was going to be hard, watching my mother deteriorate before my eyes. However, I had seen plenty of hard times over the years and handled them all successfully. Nonetheless, it wouldn't be long before I learned what hard really was. As the gatekeeper of OZ proclaimed, "This was a horse of a different color."

Eight months into my nonstop, no relief caregiving adventure, I began to experience unusual discomfort in my hands and arms followed, quite effectively, by periods of sharp pain in my chest. Being a man in my late forties (at the time), and of Sicilian pedigree with a family history that just screams heart disease, you can imagine my concern. I have always been very athletic and the thought of my heart going south seemed impossible. But everything I had heard over the years, and recently read on the Internet, suggested I should be sitting in an emergency room with a rosary in my hand and a list of apologies prepared for when Saint Peter presented himself. On top of that I wondered what would I do with mom? Although I did have family in town, it wasn't likely they would provide any assistance since I hadn't heard from them since my arrival. So I waited, prayed and made an appointment with a Cardiologist to have an EKG and get to the bottom of this frightening situation.

The EKG was negative. As a matter of fact, my heart and blood pressure were very strong. The only bad news I received on that day was I had gained thirty pounds since the move to St. Louis and not even that news prompted heart palpitations. However, while the doctor was taking one last listen to heart and lungs, mom, as if cued by God, did something unusual. The doctor heard my heart race and felt my muscles tense up and in that moment he was able to give a quick, and accurate, diagnosis, "There's your problem."

Stress is a bad "muther"...and it's unavoidable. You have got to understand, in one way or another, stress is going to show up and it's going to challenge your heart as well as your psyche. The good news is there are several ways to tame stress, all dictated by your individual situation. I can only speak for my plight, but you can take the fundamentals of what I did and how I approached stress recovery and adapt it to your own situation. Hopefully you have some support in place, someone to give you occasional breaks from the rigors of caregiving. If so, you are already a big step of the game. As I stated earlier, I was very much alone for the first year and I feel this lack of help added greatly to the stress I experienced. If it looks like you'll be alone in this endeavor, there are many groups in your community, you can turn to. As I stated, I found a wonderful adult daycare facility and, for a few dollars a week, I got to relax and mom got to interact with others, but, most importantly, she got a lot of love. In the later stages, this facility was no longer an option, but I still thank them in my daily prayers.

After my initial stress attack, I resolved to find some way to curb my problem and never let it get out of hand again. I found Las Vegas! For me, the electricity and excitement of Vegas is a great stress reliever. Couple that with the opulence found on the strip these days and you'll find one tasty recipe for "stressaseeyalater." I use all of the bells and whistles intended to distract people from their senses and hard earned cash, to divert my mind from the daily challenges I have undertaken. I know Vegas isn't for everyone, but you get the idea. Perhaps you enjoy hiking or fishing or just sitting on a beach somewhere. The point is, find something your truly enjoy and make time to do it.

I found planning the trip always began the de-stressing process. Buying tickets on-line is just the commitment necessary to alleviate a bit of that weight which sat on my shoulders. Next, I would mark the calendar with my departure date, subsequently crossing off each day leading up to my break, always focusing on the positive, keeping my eye on the goal. You will find, with each of the tasks to coordinate your trip completed, the stress is replaced with an almost euphoric sense that makes each caregiving task much more bearable. It's sort of like the Christmas spirit most of us have experience. It's not so much about the goodwill as it is about the anticipation of brotherhood and good times ahead. That's the magic which can be achieved by simply planning your getaway.

So for me, it was Vegas. Once I found it I kept it until it was no longer prudent to leave mom. When I returned from those short trips, I already had the next trip working in the back of my mind. That's the other aspect of this concept which must be practiced...the re-charge cycle. Once you return from your respite, reality is right there, the grind begins again, and it is important to have your next goal already in place. Believe me, that faint light, already glowing at the end of your next tunnel, will be just the fuel you need to be the best you can be for your loved one, but most importantly, for yourself.

YA GOTTA HAVE FAITH

Of all of the tools you bring with you on this journey, faith is by far the most important. When you're up against it, and the walls start closing in, you had better have someone, or something to rely on or you yourself will become another Alzheimer's statistic.

Spirituality of some kind must become an advocate. Whether you pray or chant, lose yourself in a yoga session, or meditate to the center of your most special place, you must have somewhere to turn. This goes beyond family and friends, they listen and they are, in most cases, important allies in the pilgrimage you are on. However, unless they are physically involved in the day-to-day routine you experience, they have no real concept of what you are going through and therefore, can only attempt to support and encourage you. Trust me, as important as all of those words of inspiration can be, you must have the security of spirituality to lean on when mere words begin to condescend.

In my case, I turned to God. I have never been a very religious person. I was raised Catholic and took the premise of Catholicism and molded it into a dogma I was comfortable with. I've been turning to that tenet for the better part of my life and can say now, with great confidence, it is the only thing which got me through 11-years of caring for mom. In order to do this thing right, you must have strength. Words of encouragement can be great motivators and reflecting on just how important your challenge is, can take you a long way. Nevertheless, you must have an ally within your psyche that can boost your morale and help get you through this enormous task you've undertaken. Prayer, and the blind faith that there is someone listening who can bestow a little boost at just the right time, in my case, was essential.

I began each day with a cup of coffee and a plea to the universe to help me face whatever might be waiting as I woke my mother and began yet another day. Believing my request would be granted gave me the strength to ascend the stairs and accept whatever surprise I might have found when I reached the top. Early on, that surprise had something to do with, for the lack of a better word, "poop." On good days, the poop was confined to the bed...those were very good days. Some mornings I was treated to the creative renderings of, "poop art," not to be confused with Pop art. The craft I refer to consists of lines and circles on walls and a very precise outline of the switch plate. Oh yes, it is quite a sight to behold considering the artist was the same woman who scolded me for scribbling on the wall with a crayon as a child. Other mornings it was just the frustration of dealing with the lethargy and confusion surrounding the most fundamental of tasks. Sitting on the toilet, stepping into the shower or brushing her teeth had become very foreign tasks to my mother. Beginning each day with this array of obstacles requires a little more than the human condition is prepared for. This was where my faith became essential. And to be honest, some morning's faith just wasn't enough and I began to ask questions of mom that would never be answered and were only responded to blankly with, "I don't know." This answer usually humbled me and curbed my frustration long enough to face the reality of the situation and exhale the building rage before it got a chance to fester inside of me. Perhaps God gave her that response in order to help me. I choose to believe that is the case and I am comfortable with my beliefs. The one thing you must remember is the answer, no matter where it came from, is the truth. **People with Alzheimer's really don't know**. If you can carry that fact in your heart, as well as your head, the task takes on a sad, but real face, and the job you have undertaken takes on a significance that just can't be measured.

There will be many times when faith fails to facilitate your situation. You will pray for help only to watch vulnerably as your predicament gains strength. During that time, I understood what

Mother Theresa must have been going through when she wrote of the absence of God she felt as she tended to the poor of Calcutta. As the peace and prosperity you so desperately request is seemingly denied by the universe, you begin to question the very faith that has been holding you together. Minor mishaps become major moments of mischief as the walls begin to close in and all of your invocations seem to fall upon deaf ears. But then, as your last fragment of faith is about to fall by the wayside, a dry diaper rejuvenates reassurance and a simple whisper from your loved one saying, "I love you," takes all of your doubt away.

Someone once said, "God works in strange and mysterious ways." I'm guessing whoever coined that phrase had a run of bad luck and, at the end of it all, found a way to survive. That's not to say God is in the habit of hanging us out to dry with the plan to pull us back in at the last minute to keep our faith alive. I don't think God plays games like that. I believe we are all in this thing alone, paving our own road and following some root of purpose. God's role, in my opinion, is to give us a nudge from time to time. It is what we do with that nudge which can make the difference between success and failure.

Anger, regret, frustration and exhaustion are all separate cars on the caregiver roller coaster you ride each day. If you attempt to ride alone, it is almost certain your car will derail and serious injury will not only befall you, but your loved one as well. Find a partner, an imaginary friend, if you will, to accompany you on the ups and downs of the everyday experiences of caring for a loved one with Alzheimer's. It will make the ride a little more interesting and the journey so much easier to complete.

HOME IS WHERE THE HEART IS

Some of my siblings held the opinion a nursing home would have been the best play in dealing with my mother. Of course, these were the same siblings who had little contact with me or mom over the course of our 11- year sojourn. I always tried to look at all sides of all opinions and gave their doubts some thought. Not a lot of thought, mind you, but some. In the event there are others out there with a similar theory, I thought it would be prudent to give a few examples, in order to show just how absurd that sort of thinking can be. This is not to say nursing homes are evil, dead places. On the contrary, many of these facilities are very pleasant, although structured and a bit regimented as they should be. What they aren't, however, is a home.

One example has to do with the unexpected visit of my older sister who, at the time, lived in Chicago. I could count on her to bring smiles to mom's and my life at least every Thanksgiving, Christmas, Mother's Day and my birthday. On one of her visits, she brought two of her friends from Chicago. One of the friends had to be in St. Louis to cover a story for a magazine and my sister found that a great opportunity to hitch a ride and spend some time with Mom and I. This was an excellent chance to have some people in the house so I invited them all to dinner on Saturday night. (One of the many upsides to my caregiving decision is, I've become quite proficient in the kitchen). Dinner was prepared and consumed and all the while laughter and conversation filled the air. Our guests were superb at directing most of their attention towards Mom and she ingested it all with a lost animation I rarely got to see. She talked and laughed and gestured comically, although she really had no idea what was being discussed. The point here is this; that scenario never would have taken place in a nursing home. I always tried to keep Mom as involved as possible, as I state in upcoming 'The Grand Illusion' chapter of this book...this night was a perfect example.

Before I continue, let me point out one very important fact. When dealing with people suffering from Alzheimer's, or any form of dementia in a group situation, it is critical that you direct as much of the laughter and conversation towards them as possible. Too many times the afflicted are talked 'at', instead of 'to,' or ignored completely. Although they have limited, if any, comprehension, the attention seems to trigger something inside of them that ignites a small flame and inspires genuine smiles. Believe me, those smiles, coming from a loved one suffering from Alzheimer's, are a rare and glorious thing.

Another example occurred sometime after the end of a holiday season. The tree was down, the decorations removed and once again it was business as usual in our home. It was one of those nights when I just wanted to spark some sort of enjoyment for my mother. As I stated earlier, the day-to-day caring of a loved one with Alzheimer's can become quite bland, especially in the evening. You've basically got television and conversation as your options. With later-stage loved ones, most of the time you've just got television. But this night I was determined to bring Mom a little joy before bedtime. After pouring myself a glass of wine, and my mother some tea in a wine glass (no more wine for her), I turned on some of the tunes she would recognize from her youth. There is something about that era of music which awakens even the darkest mind (see next Chapter). As I watched my mother become invigorated, as she seemed to recognize the tune, Swing, Swing, Swing, a request for a dance seemed appropriate. We danced and laughed and fumbled around until I could tell my mother was happily and thoroughly exhausted. A smile was frozen on her face as I prepared her for bed and a quiet, "Thank you" and "I love you" were whispered in my direction as I turned off the light. No nursing home could have given my mother that kind of pleasure. Mom had always had a little cockiness about her, especially in a social situation.

This attitude of hers was always enjoyable for me to observe, especially in my younger years. She was always so busy being a mother and housewife she seldom seemed to have any time to enjoy life. Now, Alzheimer's has all but stolen that aspect of her personality. Still, there are times, like those I have mentioned, when given the right situation, a small part of that character emerges. That, my friends, is when the marvel of caregiving explodes with love and amazement.

I'm sure there are many cases when a nursing home is the best play. However, if the 11-years I spent caring for my mother brought a bit of light to her cloudy state, and an occasional smile to her beautiful face, then for me, the caregiver roll was the ONLY play.

THAT'S ENTERTAINMENT

Of all of the marvels and mysteries surrounding Alzheimer's disease, the ability of our loved ones to remember old movies and song lyrics, is by far the most interesting. There were many days when my mother couldn't even remember her own name, but she sure did recognize Shirley Temple and Jimmy Stewart. She wasn't sure why she was sitting with me in church on Sunday, but when the music began, she knew all the lyrics.

This phenomenon can be of great use to the caregiver. Whenever I needed to throw in a load of laundry, prepare a meal or just sit in the next room and breathe, I would simply play an old movie or some big band music, and voila, instant sitter. This is also a great technique when there's a need to add some normalcy to the daily routine. As the movie plays you get an opportunity to ask questions and make comments that will, in most cases, receive a response. Now, this reply may not have anything to do with what's actually happening on the screen, but somehow the movie generates the imagination and the conversation becomes very entertaining.

Mom always had a soft spot in her heart, and for the greater part our 11-years her mind, for children. Any time we were watching Our Gang, Shirley Temple or even the early Bowery Boys films, she became very animated. Come to think of it, during the early years, she became very retrospective, as well. Visions of elementary school and the children playing on the playground, sparked memories and a soliloquy that I still have a hard time explaining. It was almost as if she was magically transported back to 1937. Perhaps the oldest memories really are the last to go. All I know is we both received a tremendous amount of joy while watching these films. Mom was probably in the most familiar, and comfortable place, left on Earth for her and I got to go along for the ride. Make sure you add movies of your loved ones youth to your collection. The experience will reaffirm the old adage, "a picture is worth a thousand words."

Music may soothe the savage beast, but it also boosts the Alzheimer's mind out of lethargy and inspires smiles and tapping toes. Certain songs can take us all back to another place, another time when love was in the air or life was just a bit more carefree. These magical melodies truly are essential when dealing with this disease. Personally, I enjoy the old tunes and when mom's foot would begin to tap to the beat, I'd often request a dance and we would 'swing' for a song or two. As the dancing concluded, and I saw that exhausted smile on my mother's face, my decision to become a caregiver was always reaffirmed.

To-date, there aren't any magic pills available to bring our loved ones back to reality; that is only a dream for the future. In the meantime, I have found the movies and music of my mother's generation are a perfect substitute for that miracle. If you want to create the most comfortable atmosphere possible for your loved one, be sure to add some of their favorite movies and music to the ingredient list on your recipe for success.

THE GRAND ILLUSION

Creating the illusion of independence is key in separating in-home care from the care our loved ones might find in a nursing home. As important as the things we do for them are, it's what we don't do for them, what we let them do themselves, (or at least attempt to do) that is the most significant. Every phase of every day provides the opportunity to ease up on the reins and allow our loved ones the chance to traverse the terrain they once dominated. As I practiced this technique, I not only motivated my mother to embrace the challenge, but set up the situation so her efforts were, more times than not, rewarded.

As the day begins, many circumstances arise that will allow you to stand back and give your loved ones the illusion of independence. Early on I would always start the shower before I woke my mother. As she got out of bed I would suggest how refreshing a shower would be and simply coax her toward the bathroom. Once there, she would usually balk a bit, but eventually step right into the shower as she had done thousands of times before. As her disease progressed, the next step of what to do once in the shower needed a little coaching, but eventually, the task was completed. Drying off was another thing that sometimes required coaxing, but most of the time she would figure it out on her own and the old routine, which is somewhat fanatic I might add, quickly came to light. Brushing her teeth was the next chore and as long as all of the tools were present, my old teacher displayed the same dental hygiene I was reluctantly taught as a child.

Eating became an opportunity with boundaries. Too many different items on a plate can be confusing, especially to a later stage Alzheimer's victim like my mother. This elementary decision making process is just too difficult and sometimes causes distress. However, an easy fix was to cut everything into bite sized portions, combine it all and present the plate to her that way. She never noticed the difference and ate happily and as her waist line showed, heartily as well. This simple adjustment allowed her to eat at her own pace with no need for instruction and eased my frustration at watching the struggle. You will find, as the disease progresses, mealtime can be quite draining for the caregiver. The person who, in many cases laid out the rudiments and fundamentals of eating to you, no longer possesses the basic skills they so lovingly shared with you in the past.

Early on, I always made sure my mother was involved when deciding the dinner menu. This simple degree of participation always seemed to lift her spirit and help her enjoy the meal a bit more. As time passed mom couldn't remember the names of any foods other than potato chips and bananas. Not being a very nutritious combination, I chose the menu for the remainder of our time together, often recreating many of the dishes she had prepared for me in hopes of triggering a memory which, unfortunately, I knew had been lost to the disease forever.

The general routine of day-to-day life can afford great opportunity to set up independent situations. Certain skills, like folding laundry, never seem to get lost in the early chaos of Alzheimer's. It always amazed me how tasks like folding towels and tying shoes can endure this disease, while loved ones names and faces get discarded.

The point of it all is simple. As a caregiver your goal is to provide the best possible world in which your loved one can live out their remaining days. Providing them with dignity and normalcy, in an atmosphere that is anything but normal, is one of the greatest gifts you can offer.

There will come a time when attempts at manipulating independence are futile. I watched my mother decline to a state that fell way beyond manipulative. At the end, I did it all. I carried her from point A to point B. I fed her, bathed her and all the time, I loved her. However, before this time arrives, it is important to allow your loved one a final, glorious opportunity to stand on their own as long as they can.

NEVER SAY NEVER

When I made the decision to care for my mother, there were certain things I was sure I couldn't, or better yet, wouldn't do. Mom had even made the statement that when she was no longer able to wipe her own butt, that it would be time for the nursing home. I had no argument with that, wiping butts was on the top of my wouldn't list. As a matter of fact, anything that had to do with seeing my mother naked was hovering around the summit of, Hell No! Prior to my arrival, mom was under the impression I was her boyfriend, coming to move in with her. This creepy thought had a great effect on my never-ever list, for I knew any unusual advance would end this endeavor before it even began. There were a few close calls...but that's a story for another time.

I think now, looking back, there is no room in the caregiver's vocabulary for the word never. Words like adapt and persevere, however, need to be highlighted and memorized.

Once you begin this journey and have invested some time and emotion, turning back becomes less and less of an option. You have got to realize you are not just giving care to your loved one. More importantly, you must be aware that you are also giving them quality of life. As this realization comes to pass, and you begin to see the profound impact your sacrifice is having, if only for brief moments, your never list begins to shrink dramatically. You see, my philosophy is this: even if she forgets the reason why, if my mother laughs or smiles or acknowledges a great tasting sandwich, those are moments I gave her, moments she may never have experienced in a nursing home.

So butt wiping was the first and most difficult obstacle. It was getting to the point where sanitation was coming into play. At first I spent a lot of time putting mom in the shower and just washing off the bulk of the mess. After a while, this became a pain in my butt, so I found a bullet, bit hard and with the aid of some Playtex gloves, began perfecting my wiping technique. Eventually this task just became a part of the daily process. I figure mom and I are *more than even* on the butt wiping duties.

They say cleanliness is next to Godliness, so in order to keep mom closer to God, I had to break another of my *nevers* and help with her bathing. Not being too sure of my mother's take on this activity, I entered with a lot of apprehension. I didn't want any confusion to trigger some sort of Alzheimer's inspired, "Hello big boy," moment. Mostly I was just a coach shouting instructions from the sidelines. Occasionally, however, there were times when I had to wash or rinse an area when my instructions were not comprehended. Eventually, for safety reasons, the shower was replaced by wet wipes, lotion and rinse free shampoo. Once again, Mom and I are more than even on the whole washing thing.

A son helping his mother with these personal tasks seems wrong on so many different levels unless you throw Alzheimer's into the equation. Then, necessity rules out all question and doubt. If I had adhered to the parameters of *never* that I had entered into, this endeavor would have never happened. Think of all of the smiles and laughter which would have been abandoned in some laugh less limbo. Even as my mother slipped deeper into the abyss of Alzheimer's, there were times when a smile or a cocky *how do ya do,* made all of the bullshit worthwhile.

PEEK - A - BOO

In the midst of all of this chaos, there will be moments when, for no logical reason, your loved one will seem to break through the fog and momentarily reflect reality. Observations will be made with a smile, verbal commands will be followed effortlessly and, it will seem some miraculous breakthrough has been made. This phenomenon will warm your heart and that small glimpse of normalcy will further inspire your mission. I had witnessed fractions of this miracle many times during my caregiving experience but on one occasion I was blown away by an incredible incident of animation, the likes of which I hadn't seen in years.

As time passed, and Alzheimer's had continued to smother my mother's spirit, the act of beginning each day had become a draining ritual of repetitive coaxing. The simple task of getting out of bed seemed to trigger conflicting signals that would ricochet inside her head like a super ball in a small room. Up is down, out is in and the disorder goes way beyond simple, morning doldrums. On this day, however, she popped out of bed smiling and responded to my question of, "How are you this morning?" with a grin, a hug, and a very coherent, I love you. As we made our way to the bathroom, she went immediately to the toilet area and sat down, still smiling and commented that, "This would be a good place to poop!"

This I mention mostly because at that stage of our journey. The simple task of sitting down had become quite a challenge for my mother. We would usually spend at least a few minutes playing an unconventional game of charades, where I would go through the squatting motion of sitting down, all the while coaxing her to mimic me. On this day, the game was called, due to coherency.

Moving on to the shower, I was again taken by surprise as my mother effortlessly stepped into the tub. Normally we spent a lot of time just trying to figure out the first step. She would reach for the soap, feet firmly planted on the tile floor and somehow she equated that with stepping into the shower. Eventually, I would employ the fundamentals of a trick I took from Jason Lee and Julia Stiles in the movie, **A Guy Thing**. I would step into the shower, mom would follow and I would slide the door closed on one end and exit from the other side, leaving her safely ready for the morning spritz. You must be creative with this disease and take your inspiration from wherever you can get it. In any event, on this occasion, all aspects of the shower experience were performed cleanly.

Throughout this entire time, there was also an animated, yet unconventional, conversation going on between us. I normally didn't share in conversation most mornings unless I received a phone call. I was usually drained by the time we finally reached the breakfast table and needed a few minutes to recharge before attempting the usual panned banter that was common between my mother and me. On this day, the words coming out of her mouth were better than the lyrics of any Lennon and McCartney song. She commented on the color of her sweater, read the Kansas City Chiefs logo on my shirt and couldn't get over how beautiful our living room was. The point is, for the first time in a very long time, there were two voices in our home.

On that particular day Mom was slated to spend some time at the adult daycare facility I spoke of earlier. Normally that's a ride where I ask a lot of questions, hoping to inspire conversation. Most of the time there was no response and mom lethargically stared out the window. Not on this day. She was reading stop signs, noticing school buses and commenting on the children riding in them. It was a cold morning and I mentioned Christmas was right around the corner and if, on cue, she began a rousing rendition of Jingle Bells. I welled up a bit and joined in at the chorus, singing happily for almost a mile. Then, the most miraculous thing happened...she knew where we were going! Before the hospital that housed the facility even came into view, she commented on how much fun she had there and that she wanted me to come in with her. "I'm your mother," she said smiling, "And I just want to know that you're going to be ok." Tears could not be contained after that bombshell and I will never be too proud to admit it. I can't explain this phenomenon and frankly I don't care to. It was a great moment in a world that sorely lacked great moments.

When I picked up mom that afternoon, it was back to business as usual. Mumbling replaced words, the distant stare had returned and the ride home was quite different than that of our miraculous morning. Nonetheless, it was a fantastic day. I was rewarded for my patience and tenacity with a short trip on a time machine. I enjoyed that day away more than most and, for the first time since my last trip to Las Vegas, I looked forward to getting back to caring for my mother.

If you are currently caring for someone with Alzheimer's disease, be on the lookout. You will see fragments of reality, daily. These moments range from the ability of your loved one to tie a shoe and sing a song, all the way across the spectrum to the ability to recognize a face or acknowledge the taste of a favorite meal. But when you have the opportunity to experience a day like I had, relish it. A day like that is a lot like milk, it does a body good.

A note of caution must be made here. However glorious her brief rendezvous with reality appeared, it was only an aberration. Take joy in the moment but do not let this brief departure from the norm cloud your perception of reality. I found myself getting frustrated with the return to our normal existence following many of these events. It is important to stay focused on the disease. Be thankful for the reprieve but look beyond it and rest on the knowledge your loved one still resides somewhere in that dark room which has become their home.

OPPORTUNITY DETOURED

My mother never had the chance to become a cute, little old lady. She was very cute and she was definitely old, but Alzheimer's disease stole the package one thinks of concerning *cute little old ladies* from her. She was well on her way to full, cute status when the disease decided to derail her ascension. Occasionally I would see a glimmer of cuteness, but those moments were sorrowfully overshadowed by the dissonance that had consumed her.

When I think of *cute little old ladies*, I see a swarm of red hats entering a casino for a day out with the girls. I envision a table at a local restaurant where glasses are clinking and the accomplishment of age, like a badge of honor, glows from the faces sitting there. I see a grandmother savoring another holiday with children and grandchildren, soaking up the moments while still keeping everyone in line. I see survivors who have faced all that life has thrown at them and now relish it in an almost mystical way. Sometimes, my imagination sees my mother there and the injustice of it all is what fuels my tenacity.

On many occasions I find myself envying those cute little old ladies on behalf of my mother. I don't resent them for what they have. On the contrary, I enjoy the spectacle of it all and when the opportunity presents itself, I usually find a way to applaud them. But as I retreat from these encounters, I can't help but feel a bit melancholy, always struggling with the idea that my mother would never again be part of that world.

I think I experienced more sorrow from seeing this aspect of her life extinguished than I did when I would dwell on the many missed opportunities this disease took from me. God willing, I will have plenty of chances to grow old and continue to experience the passion, excitement and adventure of life. For my mother, opportunity was a gift that, as a caregiver, I gave in the form of an impromptu dance or a sing-along to a special song that somehow found a glow in the darkness of her mind. You see, when you boil it all down, that is what being a caregiver is all about. It's not the cleaning and feeding that is our ultimate goal, it's the opportunity we give our loved ones to occasionally grasp reality. In a world I can only imagine to be surreal at best, we provide normalcy in an abnormal atmosphere. We provide comfort and familiarity to a person living in a foreign fog. We represent the only light in a world going from dusk to dark in a hurry.

UNREGRETABLE

People often ask if there are times when I regret the decision I made. I will admit there were many moments when I wondered what the hell I was thinking, but one look into my mother's eyes always answered that question. As far as regret goes, however, there has never been a single moment. But as I think of regret, that horrendous hell of hindsight we've all experienced, I reflect on those regrettable moments and wonder now if the regrets weren't just pre-determined detours in my life that had to occur in order for me to become my mother's caregiver.

Strangely enough, my first true regret occurred just weeks before my second regret, the one that seems to have set this whole play in motion. The date was May 16, 1976; it was a Sunday afternoon and I ended an argument with my father by screaming, "Just leave me alone!" On May 17, 1976, my father died and I never got the chance to take those words back. Regret with big bold letters. During my father's funeral, a very dear friend of his informed me I was the man of the family now and it was my duty to look after my mother and two younger siblings. What? I was a week away from High School graduation and a summer away from college and freedom. This was not the kind of pressure I needed at this juncture of my life. This was not the kind of responsibility a teenager can, or should, have to handle. This was the decision I would make that would be the first of a series of events which had to occur in order for me to arrive in St. Louis and become the caregiver for my mother.

So college, and the magic world I had hoped to find there, was placed on hold. Instead, I joined the ranks of the working folk at my father's business. I always hated that place but the guilt of our argument, and some deep rooted feelings of obligation, lead me through those doors every day. At some point I realized I really wasn't looking after anyone, including myself. As I continued to go through the motions of a teenage working man, I began praying for some way out. Shortly after, God answered my prayers by guiding two cars into the rear of my Ford LTD and that glorious sign from above, in the form of back trauma, was enough to get me the hell out of there.

Now doesn't that sound like a regrettable situation? Maybe, but if none of those things had occurred, and I had gone to college like I'd planned, I would have never discovered my innate talent for the sport of racquetball. I made a short career out of the sport and was ascending towards great things. However, while preparing for a big tournament, my ankle found a hole in a steep hill I was running and two breaks and some ligament damage later, put an abrupt end to that dream. I could, and do regret, hitting the hill that day but if that tragic moment hadn't occurred, I never would have met one of the best friends I have ever had. Sidelined by the injury, I followed that friend into the strange world of small town America. I gained a true appreciation for how genuinely friendly and sincere people can be and received an education in humanity I may never have had the opportunity had none of those earlier regrets occurred. Eventually, it was time for me to move on, begin my education and set course for the final chain of events that had to occur in order for me to be writing these words today.

In keeping with my newfound appreciation for small town America, I enrolled at Pittsburg State University. Not in Pennsylvania, they need the H to complete their name. This small collegiate gem is located in the State of Kansas, just north of the small Missouri town I had been residing. I rediscovered my love of writing there, but more importantly, I met the future mother of my daughter. Truly that daughter is reason enough to have no regrets about the past. Having said that, if my marriage had worked out, the possibility of me being able to care for mom doesn't even exist. I followed that woman to the most dreaded place on earth for me at the time, Kansas City. The Royals had recently stolen a world championship from my beloved Cardinals and that town made me ill. Had I not made that move, however, I would never have met three of the most significant people who have entered my life and, of course, I wouldn't have lost them either. Also, I would never have found the home of my heart and the greatest little town on earth. Still will never be a Royals fan though.

The point here is simple. If any of my life's regrets had not occurred, chances are I would not have been in a position to drop it all and take care of my mother. So, when I'm asked the question of regret, I can ponder and reflect and smile for as much as I've lost I have gained tenfold with the opportunity to care for my mother.

ZIPPERS AND BUTTONS AND STRINGS, OH MY!

There is going to come a time when the type of clothing your loved one wears will have to change. Early on in my experience, mom went through the *destruction phase.* This bizarre ritual found my mother ripping and gnawing at her blouses, nightgowns and slacks. I can only guess she was under the impression that they were new clothes and she was simply removing the price tags. In reality, she was tearing at the mfg tags, sometimes with her teeth and subsequently ripping the back off of her shirts, pants and sleepwear. Her feline instincts also matured at this time and she developed a kitten-like fascination with string. Loose thread on pillows, blankets and quilts, were helpless against her fanatic fingers. One morning I woke to find my mother centered within a pile of feathers, string and the lifeless carcass of a once respected down comforter. Needless to say, the frustration of these episodes prompted an urgent need for change.

The first step I took was to remove all of the non-essential clothing, extra quilts and unnecessary furniture from her room. She really only slept and napped there and the comfort of the familiar had lost much of its significance where mom was concerned. In the beginning I felt it was important to keep everything as familiar as possible in order to maintain order and ease the confusion that a move can bring. Now, however, recognition of a piece of furniture, a favorite sweater or even the face of her son was a stretch. I took all of her remaining clothes and inspected each item for tags, loose thread, etc. I removed the tags, cut the thread and prayed that I had done enough.

Secondly, when purchasing new clothes, I looked for shirts without tags. Many manufacturers now print their label right on the material. I bought slacks with elastic waistbands so as to avoid the button, zipper dilemma. I was also confronted with the constant zipping and buttoning that unsure hands seem to gravitate. Also, her doctor suggested that mom gain some weight (in case of a fall, etc.) so the flexible waistband came in real handy. Of all of these idiosyncrasies, the snapping of buttons and the constant ups and downs of a zipper are the closest thing to fingernails on a chalkboard that I dealt with. The seasons of winter, spring and fall, magical times of football and the beginning, and end, of baseball have now become times I dread, for these are the times of coats and jackets, all of which have buttons and zippers.

Also included in this exercise of destruction are the tearing and folding of paper, most notably, magazines and their pages.

Remember also to inform family members and friends of this new list of clothing criteria. Clothing is a popular gift idea and this simple request will keep you away from frustrating return lines.

REASONS

The choice I made, and the subsequent path my decision had set me on, inspired observations from onlookers which included, saintly, heroic and extraordinary. Many people commented that because of the commitment I had made, the bond between my mother and I must have been the stuff of legend. Beaver and June Cleaver, Greg and Carol Brady or even Alice and Tommy Hyatt, all came to mind when I heard this praise. Generally I would smile and nod in agreement while allowing this myth to live on. However, in my mind's eye, nothing could be further from the truth...almost.

I was born prematurely, exiting my mother's womb in the summer of 1957. My lungs hadn't fully developed and as a result, I spent my first days on this earth in an incubator. I'm not sure how many days I lay there pondering whatever thoughts a newborn ponders, because no one I know really remembers. However, I did surmise it was at least a week and am convinced my claustrophobia is a direct result of the time I spent there. The one thing I do know for certain about the time is, I spent at least some of it alone. You see, my mother left me in a glass box at DePaul hospital and went home. Technology and germs had not yet caught up with each other so with my quasi-quarantine on, there was no reason for her to spend time in a foreign bed. I assume she visited me daily, but when you boil it down, I was left alone in the care of strangers. It's ironic how the tables had turned on us.

The history of my mother and I began on that warm July morning. How happy she must have been bringing her third child into the world. Actually, it was 4:30 a.m.; so happy might not be the appropriate term. In those days my sex was still a mystery but if I came out with proper equipment, I was to be named after my father. Traditionally the first-born Sicilian son is given his father's name but a wartime promise made by my father, to a fellow soldier somewhere in France, changed all of that. I understand there was quite a riff over that decision and, since my parent's second child was a girl, my Sicilian grandparents had to wait nine years before the tradition was to continue.

The earliest memories of my mother are obscure at best. What I do remember first and foremost is she appeared different than all of the other mothers I came in contact with; she seemed older somehow, a little more worn and a bit obtuse. Her instincts as a mother were present but she seemed to be lacking in the basic rudiments and fundamentals of actually being a mom. I remember she never really took charge of any daily conflicts concerning the kids and always waited for my father to come home to drop those bombs. She did follow the mother/wife rule book as far as the daily routine was concerned. For example, I never went a day without a balanced breakfast and a well rounded packed lunch. She did her best to create dinners that, although common in our home, were considered special by the occasional friend who would stay over. I was always as clean, if not cleaner, than all the other kids. I was well-groomed, dressed smartly and was given an early education in manners and etiquette that I still utilize today. My mother did all of this with no real example to fall back on.

When she was very young, mom's father died of pneumonia. There were also three younger brothers in her house and the economy of the mid 1930's caused my grandmother to make the difficult decision to let others raise her children. Fortunately my grandfather was a Mason and my grandmother placed her four children in the charitable hands of the Masonic Home and sought work in order to survive. This single situation in my mother's life was pivotal in my decision to keep her at home as long as possible.

Mom and her siblings would spend an occasional weekend or holiday with their mother. However, when you boil it all down, the Masons raised her and her brothers. With this situation in play, my mother never had the opportunity to observe her own mother routinely managing a household and raising children. Subsequently she was a true novice when it came to dealing with our family situation. Mom resided in the Masonic Home until her senior year in high school. At that time the Masons had arranged a scholarship for her to the Julliard School in New York. It seems that singing voice I cringed at while sitting in church on Sundays was really quite unique. She passed on that opportunity in order to finally spend some time with her mother. There have surely been times when that decision was regretted, but mom played the cards life dealt her and I think she was at least content with the way her hand played out.

Most children of my generation had a mother waiting at home for them at the end of each school day. As a very young child I recall looking forward to getting back to that base and feeling the comfort and safety of mom and home. There were never cookies and milk waiting, or even an interested ear as to the events of my day, but she was there and, at that time, it was enough.

In our house, to quote Dickens, "It was the best of times, it was the worst of times." We always had the best food, clothing, toys and stuff in general that was available. We got central air conditioning before anyone else, we had the first color TV on the block, we had nice cars and all the material things a kid could ask for. What was lacking in our home was love.

In order for me to truly explain my relationship with my mother and my decision to become her caregiver, it is necessary, and a bit awkward, for me to expound on my father and the environment we all grew up in.

My father was one of six sons of immigrant parents, fresh off the boat from Sicily. Although the emphasis on family is prevalent in Sicilian lore, in their case it was a tough love...rarely displayed openly, but somehow taken for granted to be present. I can only imagine the insanity that must have hovered in their household. If the dynamic of that family was ever replicated on a reality TV show, it would probably be entertaining, but ultimately viewed as a depressing example of dysfunction fueled by a strong surge of culture shock. Unlike my mother, my father did have an example of parenting to draw from...unfortunately it was a very bad example.

Again, I bring up my father's history only to set up the atmosphere of our household and further explain the reasoning behind my decision to care for my mother. Don't get me wrong; my father was a good man. As a matter of fact, there are many people who would even go so far as to say he was a great man. Strangely enough, as I now reflect on it, I would be one of those people. But, to say he was a good father or husband would be a lie.

Fun stopped when my father entered the room. Actually, fun stopped when we heard him pull into the driveway. Eggshells always appeared on the floor when he arrived and that was no way for children to perceive a parent. I can't even imagine what my mother must have gone through dealing with this moody, unpredictable man every day for so many years. It is the fact that she somehow persevered this dilemma, as well as the many other detours of her life, that garnered her the respect, in my eyes, that would warrant this small sacrifice I have undertaken.

Sometimes, when I felt the walls closing in on me, I thought back to the situation my mother founder herself and I could truly sympathize with her. However, I do know what causes the confusion I deal with. It's a defined disease, with basic guidelines I can follow and deal with. She is dealing with a time bomb that had no ticking clock counting down to detonation. Mom must have always been waiting for the spark that would set off my father and, if for no other reason, that torturous situation always had my empathy, love and appreciation.

Being the third of five children, and having a span of nine years between my older brother, and six years between my older sister, there really wasn't anyone for me to hang out with early on in our house. Fortunately, we grew up in a neighborhood with an abundance of children in or around my age group. There was an elementary school across the street with a playground, basketball courts and two baseball fields. Mom was more than willing to allow me the freedom to explore all that the neighborhood had to offer. This was the time I began to hone my athletic skills and started realizing the positive aspects of becoming proficient at as many sports as possible. As the years passed, and I was getting more and more involved in the local organized sports scene, I had found a way to stand out, make friends and, most importantly, stay out of the house.

As I advanced deeper into the sanctuary that sports provided, a bond somehow began to grow between my mother and me. The indifference I perceived in her began to transform into an interest, which, at times, exceeded that of many of the other parents. I guess the light that began to shine on me enticed some latent desires within my mother. Early on I only had teammates and coaches to look to for inspiration. Other kid's parents would congratulate me and applaud outstanding play when my parents weren't there. I remember many times gazing in vain towards the stands or the sidelines hoping to see my mother or father rooting me on. The disappointment of those moments began to mold a protective vein of coldness in me and form a facade of indifference I struggle with to this day.

But then I began to see my mother there. At first she would just sit alone trying to figure out the how's and why's of the event. Eventually, other moms would entice her to join them and her addiction in my escape began. Once quiet rides to and from practices and games where now filled with questions and preparatory remarks that were both confounding and comforting. For the first time since this woman gave birth to me, we were beginning to bond. Perhaps that time in the incubator affected us both and the inevitable was finally coming to light.

There are two specific moments I will always remember that went a long way in helping me decide to become my mother's caregiver. The first was during my freshman year in high school. My kidney was bruised in the course of a football game and, while I was lying on the ground reeling in pain and uncertainty, I could hear my mother scream with concern from the stands. I remember begging my teammates to keep her off the field and did my best to make it to my feet and act unscathed. It sounds odd, but this was the first time it really seemed my mother truly cared about me. Blood coming from the wrong places prompted a trip to the hospital where mom sat with me doing her best to encourage me and keep me calm. This would seem the end to this memorable tale but it only sets it up.

When I returned home I was sitting uncomfortably at the kitchen table attempting to eat some dinner. My father entered the room and began belittling me for slouching at the table. Normally this behavior would go unnoticed at our house, but not this evening. For the first time in the history of me, and probably time, my mother scolded my father and bravely stood up for me, explaining the events of the early evening. Silence and apprehension followed her noble stand as all eyes were on my father. No one really knew what to do at that point and dad just quietly made his way towards the basement. Nothing else was ever said about it, but that unique moment was stamped in the forefront of my memory and will remain there forever.

The other memorable mom moment came in the form of a routine. From the time I was seven or eight years old I spent every summer competing in both baseball and swimming. This story involves swimming. For some reason my mother got it in her head that in order for me to perform at my peek, there were three things I needed before each swim meet: a medium rare T-bone steak, very sweet iced tea and a Bit-O-Honey candy bar. I'm not sure where she got the idea, but believe me, I never complained. Some weeks I would compete in two or three meets and that pre-event meal was always there. But more importantly than the food, I remember my mother sitting there with me. I can't remember specific topics of conversation, but I do remember feeling a special bond that was uniquely ours. I also remember my siblings questioning why I got such special treatment and enjoying the rush of uniqueness that their jealousy fed to me. Those times are some of the most vivid early memories I have of my mother and I pray I never forget them.

Times slowly passed and with it my priorities began to shift from sports and girls to college and girls. Finally, I could see that dim light of escape at the end of the proverbial tunnel begin to glow. It was as if I had my hand firmly gripped on the brass ring of freedom and all I needed was the strength of time to pull it into my possession. Who I was and who I was going to become was not little more than a summer away. Mom was both supportive and aloof during this time. My father wanted me to stay close to home but I had someplace just a bit further to the east of center in mind. Mom seemed to understand my need for distance, although she could never share that philosophy with my father. Contradiction was not something he took lightly. I think she was living vicariously through my quest for enlightenment and escape.

As I got older, the inquisitor that lived in the soul of my mother showed herself from time to time. Rudimentary questions about everything from the topics I wrote about, to the words I chose to read, were asked with a sincerity that only now can I truly comprehend. In those days I was certain there was an ulterior motives to her interest. Perhaps she thought it all had to do with drugs; after all I was reading Herman Hesse and Carlos Constenada in junior high. A few glances at those works by an unknowing eye could lead to any number of conclusions. But her interest was true. Pent up desires, and deflated dreams, prompted occasional appearances from the *inner mom*, and those visits drew both my respect and my sympathy.

As I became more aware of my own surroundings, and myself, I also became more in tune with the daily conflicts and struggles that my mother had to deal with. I now saw this woman, who I had taken for granted most of my life, as an unfinished work of art. A clay pot that had been molded and designed but never sent to the kiln for firing. I saw nothing and I saw everything, all wrapped up in the package that was my mother. We never really talked about that aspect of life and at the time I never acknowledged my observations. I guess I was just too busy holding on to that ring and keeping my eye focused on the light

For a while there was an entirely new dynamic between my mother and me. For reasons I explained in an previous chapter, I suddenly became the man of the house. In reality, I was not a man at all being only seventeen at the time, but I attempted to live up to the role anyway. You would think this would be an opportunity for my mother and me to grow even closer. Instead it became a chaotic charade that overwhelmed me and I was forced to cut away the psychological bindings that held me there and abruptly move on. My mother, cutting me off from everything from the front door key to college tuition, made threats of desperation in hopes of dissuading me from moving out of the house. However, I could feel my sanity slowly slipping away and these threats seemed a small price to pay.

Eventually we sorted it all out and I went off into the world and mom stood behind me almost every step of the way. This is when our relationship went to a place that would eventually lead back to her door.

For the longest time it seemed as if I was traveling through life with a man named Murphy. As soon as I found success on a chosen path, something always seemed to find a way to obscure the road and detour my efforts. Most of the time I managed to rob Peter to pay Paul but on those occasions when Peter and I were both tapped out, my mother was always there to help keep the boat afloat. With all of the sentimental reasons I had for taking care of her, it was this sense of debt that significantly fueled my decision.

During my years away, a strange thing happened to my mother, she finally blossomed. After years of sitting dormant and struggling just to maintain mediocrity, Mary Betty LaRico's roots finally found fertile soil. She mourned my father's death for several years and managed to maintain the house and raise my younger two siblings. Eventually she began to date. Finally she met a guy named Bill. Soon after, I began receiving postcards from faraway lands and I couldn't believe my mother was exploring them. Morocco, Alaska, Vegas and on and on and on. I hadn't met Bill but from what I could surmise, he was the perfect match for my mother. There were pictures of my mother holding a stringer full of fish...that she'd caught! This was not the Mary Betty LaRico I knew. This woman was no longer just Mary Betty LaRico, but simply and elegantly, Mary. I can't convey to you how wonderful this transformation was. Hell, she even had sun bleached hair and a tan! My mother had become the woman that she was always meant to be. She was alive with confidence and personality the likes of which I had never seen before and I was ecstatic. Bill spoiled my mother in every way and I wish now I had the chance to thank him.

A few years into their relationship Bill suffered a stroke and lost his ability to walk. My mother became his caregiver, wheeling him around, changing him, cleaning him and staying by his side. They still went on the occasional cruise, but eventually Bill succumbed to his condition and we lost him. Whenever I think of my mother in those pre-Alzheimer's days, I always smile, apologize to my father, and thank God for Bill.

Soon after Bill passed, mom was diagnosed with Alzheimer's. I believe the first indicator was a bad batch of meatballs. In any event, the glorious life she had finally experienced was now going to be dissolved and this, above all else, is the reason I decided to care for her. She deserved more time and the only way I could insure that was to give her some of mine.

A FUNNY THING HAPPENED ON THE WAY HOME FROM THE HOSPITAL

It was a typical Sunday morning, I was dragging myself up the stairs, praying for some relief and craving that first cup of coffee. Many mornings I'd attempt to bargain with God over a hot cup of Joe in hopes of some simple rest or reward in the middle of all of this chaos. Today I just wanted some time off. Free hours become a precious and significant fuel source that can sustain you on this journey. As I began the final ascent towards mom's room, I heard the most unusual snoring sound and smiled at the apparent humor of it. Upon entering my mother's bedroom the smile on my face was quickly replaced by the tight lips of fear and concern. She was curled up on her bed, wheezing and exhaling with a force that pushed her lips with vibration that only replicated a snoring sound. Her eyes were rolled up in the corner of their sockets and were non-responsive as I tried to verbally catch her attention. Three seconds of panic told me this was something I wasn't prepared to deal with and dialing 911 was my only option. This was not the kind of time off I was looking for.

For the first time since this adventure had begun I was unable to help my mother and keep her from harm's way. The paramedics and fire department came blazing to the rescue within minutes of my call. I led them to my mother, still curled up in urine soaked sheets, wheezing and looking very puny and fragile. A few questions and some quick tests gave our rescuers all the information they needed and as they maneuvered my mother to a stretcher they assured me that all would be okay. I secured the house and followed them to the hospital behind some of the worst drivers in driving history. Of course they were probably fine drivers but this sense of urgency I was experiencing seemed to trigger every red light and slow down every driver in my path. Nonetheless, I made my way to the hospital in a fog of cursing and complaining, all the while finding time for prayers. Only a Catholic could do both.

The technical term was T.I.A. (Transient Ischemic Attack), a small stroke caused by a temporary loss of blood flow to the brain. The term I used at the time was full of expletives cloaked in the hope I never again had to witness anything this horrific. In any event, we spent the better part of Saturday in the E.R. Mom was very non-responsive during this time and all I could do was hold her hand, stroke her hair and tell her that I loved her. The helplessness one experiences while falling victim to the ordered chaos of an emergency room is overwhelming. Thank God for cell phones and vending machines, for without them I would have melted in the mayhem. I was able to inform all immediate family of the situation and, although I wasn't yet sure of the diagnosis, I had the better part of an assumption that all was not going to end this weekend. Actually, this tragedy brought my two brothers to my aid for the first time since I arrived in St. Louis. It was nice to experience the sensation, however short-lived it might have been. Nine hours after being brought to the hospital mom was finally admitted. As I watched them transfer my mother's limp body to her new bed I dreaded the worse for our future.

As the final tube was secured and the doctors dropped by to fill me in on the series of steps that would be taken in order to complete their diagnosis, I found a moment to exhale. It seemed as if I had been holding my breath all day. I was now convinced my mother was in competent hands and I could breathe again. I sat by my mother's side, still holding her hand, still attempting conversation and still assuring her I was there and I loved her. At some point I realized I was exhausted, hungry and unable to help anyone by sitting in that room a minute longer. Convinced by the nurse that there was no guilt in retreat, I kissed mom's forehead and went home. It would be a lie if I said the better part of me didn't enjoy time alone in the home. In the four years since we had lived there I hadn't had many alone moments there. Once I got settled and took a long hot shower I realized that the last thing I wanted to do was sit at home. This was an opportunity to get out and taste a bit of the life I rarely experienced. I took myself to dinner, visited a local casino and mingled amongst the living for the first time in months. Although the plight of my mother was firmly planted in the back of my brain, I had done all I could do for her and a small slice of living was just what I needed at the moment.

Sunday morning I woke up alone and as much as I wanted to continue this holiday, my mother was also lying alone in a hospital room and with that thought, I quickly returned to her. When I arrived she had just gone down for some tests so I had the hospitals version of coffee in the lounge, watched Bob Villa build a modular house on the television and silently prayed that all would be ok. When mom finally returned, she appeared unchanged from the night before. I'm not sure what I expected, but her condition seemed to exaggerate the dread that was hovering within my psyche. The nurses and doctors all seemed optimistic and I took them at their word while spending the day watching television and continuing my barrage of prayers. The day ended as uneventfully as it began and I returned home that evening carrying continued concern for the future.

Monday morning I entered my mother's room and found her sitting in a chair with a magazine in her hands and her eyes focused on the television. "Good morning, dear," was spoken with a smile as she noticed me enter the room. Somehow she possessed more clarity and animations than I've seen or heard in years. We had many quasi conversations during the course of the day and I was taken aback by this apparent miracle. She was discharged that evening and with the final doctor's orders in hand, it was clear to me that the beginning of an unbelievable detour to our journey had just begun.

It's a funny thing about detours; more often than not you take them blindly, uncertain of the road ahead, driving cautiously and trusting that the signs will return you to your path. This was no exception. The ride home from the hospital was surreal. Observations of traffic, children in cars and billboards by my mother set the pace for a future that, for a time, had been both remarkable and frustrating. It was confounding that a tragedy, such as a stroke, could somehow rearrange her brain cells and, although she was by no means cured, my mother was much more observant and extremely more talkative. At first I marveled at this change in the landscape of our journey. Just to have another active voice in the house was somewhat refreshing. However, as time passes and the uniqueness of the chatter began to wear off, the frustration of non-stop rambling began to take its toll. Sometimes I would intercept the conversation she was having with her quixotic audience and try to steer it towards something that resembles coherency. Other times I would just go with the flow and marvel at the animation and sincerity of her direction. There are also times when the day is drawing to a close and the dueling conversations between my mother and our friends on the television attack the last nerve I have available and I must plead with my mother for a bit of quiet time and attempt to divert her attention away from the windmills and on to a moment or two of solitude.

A DAY IN THE LIFE

As I hear the ocean waves crash against the shore, I'm reminded once again of the reality of my plight. Of course, since I live in St. Louis, Missouri, the thunder of those waves is being generated by the "nature sounds" of my Timex digital alarm clock. Some mornings I'm greeted by the call of birds chirping but I find those simulated wave sounds to be just obnoxious enough to force me to quickly stretch for the off button. It's 6:00 a.m. and, although I've been awake for awhile now, that sound beacons yet another day of caring for my mother who suffers from Alzheimer's disease. Actually, today is day 1,367 of my quest and just getting out of bed each morning is becoming more and more of a Herculean task.

Some mornings I succumb to the power of procrastination and push my exit from what seems the only safe place in our home all the way up to 7:00 a.m. knowing full-well my extra hour of psychological preparation will probably lead to mom soiling her sheets, but some mornings I just don't give a damn. This morning was one of those mornings. I grabbed the remote and started surfing the music video channels on the television. I usually request of the universe a particular artist and when, and if, that artist appears, I take it as a sign of good things to come and exit my bed to start the day. This might sound a bit juvenile, but at this point I do whatever it takes to get me motivated. This morning I was looking for the Dixie Chicks. With those girls you were once able to hedge your bet a bit because they could be found on the country channels as well has VH-1 and MTV, but since that infamous statement by Natalie Maines, the country stations were now a real gamble. Freedom of speech should never be a tricky privilege, but America can sometimes be a tricky place. In any event, today it was VH-1. The Chicks weren't - *ready to make nice* and at only 6:34 a.m., I still wasn't ready to get out of bed. As my mind quickly began concocting ways to rationalize staying in bed a bit longer, I took the prudent route because, as far as I was concerned, a deal with the universe is a deal I really didn't want to break, so out of bed I slowly rose.

Donning some sweat pants and a Kansas City Chiefs T-shirt, I cracked my neck, moaned out an exaggerated exhale and began to ascend the 12-steps that led to my first two stops of the morning; the kitchen and the bathroom, in that order. I have become a man of routines. It is imperative that I start my coffee brewing before any other task of the day is attempted. Some mornings the urge to reverse this routine is strong, if you know what I mean, but it seems that in order to insure a successful day, I must always make the kitchen the first priority.

Staring at the aging face in the mirror, I splash it with some warm water and then wash it with soap I have collected from my trips to Las Vegas. Somehow the smell of Mandalay Bay inspires me to persevere. Those olfactory senses always take me back, if only briefly, to the one place that had been my haven during all of this. The power of taste and smell never fail to astonish me. In any event, I dry my face, brush my teeth and head back to the kitchen for that first cup of coffee - Columbian with just a hint of Hazelnut - to savor my last moments of solitude.

I take the coffee to the living room, turn on the lamp and line up all the remotes required to get the day started. I'm tempted to relax a bit and catch a few minutes of CNN, but duty does call and instead I turn to channel 801 on my Direct-TV receiver and the golden sounds of the forties fill the room. This is the music of my mother's era and, although she rarely acknowledges Sammy Kay or Benny Goodman, I play it each morning in the hopes of jogging a brief memory. With that task complete, I savor one more sip of the hot java and then ascend the next flight of twelve steps as the reality of my life begins to take hold.

I've installed a gate at the top landing in order to keep mom in and detour her from the stairs. She has access to the bathroom even though she doesn't have the ability to get there anymore. I throw one final prayer to the heavens and enter my mother's room. I'm greeted there with a hushed "Good morning," and, as I began to raise the blinds, I am once again witness to the unusual senseless stammering that somehow has replaced conversation in our home. Today it had something to do with the pretty ladies, babies, goats and someone named Bobby. Mom had a brother named Bobby who died when he was just an infant. The circumstance of his death is not clear, but family lore has it that mom pushed him out of a window. Actually, I'm not sure how valid that is and, quite frankly, it isn't something I want to know one way or another.

With the blinds up I noticed the snow storm which was predicted had yet to appear, but the gloomy skies told me it wasn't far off as they allowed on a bit of additional light into the room. I pulled the bed spread and sheets from my mother's curled body and was elated at what I uncovered...dry sheet! It's amazing all the things that make me happy these days. Dry sheets in the morning are at the top of that list. I'm not sure where she stores all that urine but most mornings her Depends® are not dependable enough to hold it all. Subsequently, I do a lot of laundry and change a lot of sheets. If all else fails, I'm sure I could get a housekeeping job with one of the local hotels.

As mom lays motionless in that same curled position, the first frustrating event of my day prepares to unfold. I request she gets out of bed and she responds with a hushed, "Yeah," and moves nary a muscle. I then begin repeating my request, changing the inflection of my voice to animating and promising everything from money to French toast in an attempt to get her to respond. The confusion and uncertainty on her face is heartbreaking. It's as if she knows a response is in order, but the signal gets lost almost as quickly as it is heard.

Eventually she rises from her slumber and slowly scoots her butt off the side of the bed. As she stands, a stunted smile comes to her face as if she is just seeing something for the first time. "Good morning," is again whispered and the story of the goat and the pretty ladies is resurrected.

With the task of getting her out of bed accomplished, it is now time for the second hurdle of the morning ritual...getting from point A to point B. I always make the request first and, some mornings, she at least walks in the general direction of the bathroom. Today she just stands there. Her faint smile disappears and a blank stare of confusion takes its place. Unlike getting out of bed, leading her to the bathroom is as simple as taking her hand and showing her the way. Actually, I see the third, fourth and fifth hurdle all lined up one after the other. I have become the Edwin Moses of this event but the frustration still cuts deep into my psyche.

Still wanting her to do for herself as much as possible, I request she remove her clothes. Some mornings this event takes longer than others. Today was going to be a long day. Her response to my request was the same as her response to almost every request anymore, "Yeah." It's the craziest thing I have ever witnessed. Picture Rain Man on Quaaludes and you might begin to understand. Eventually I remove her clothing and am immediately faced with the fourth hurdle; getting her to sit on the toilet. This again goes on and on until eventually she seems to completely understand my request and promptly sits down. I still haven't figured out a safe way to speed up the process and remain ever patient in my duty.

The final hurdle of the morning, at least this aspect of the morning, is getting her to step into the tub. Today this task took all of five minutes. After much balking on her part, I finally stepped into the tub, led her in behind me, and then exited through the other end. The tactic is always successful and I should probably just do it right away.

However, as I said, I still like to at least let her attempt things on her own and use this tactic as a last resort. In any event, I adjust the temperature of the water, turn on the shower and pray the soaking I will soon receive is minimal. Since she no longer has a firm grasp on anything resembling reality, I must reach in from the shower end of the tub and direct the spray to her entire body hoping today she will be able to at least wash herself on her own. I direct her towards the soap; she takes it in her hand, shows it to me, and repeats the word, "Soap," and smiles while actually beginning to wash up. This is a great relief for me. Normally she just stands there, unsure of what the next move should be and I end up washing her and getting drenched in the process. With a sigh of relief I point the shower-head towards her sudsy body and begin the final leap of the morning by rinsing her off.

Once out of the shower I don't even attempt to have her dry herself. It is much easier, and a lot quicker, not to mention more efficient, if I just do it myself. With this task complete, it is simply a matter of loading up her tooth brush, standing her in front of the mirror and watching her perform the one task she still hasn't forgotten. With teeth fresh and clean, I simply slip on her Depends and dress her for the day ahead. What a way to start the day!

Some mornings we go straight to the kitchen where I help her into her chair, comb her hair and attempt conversation while I prepare breakfast. This morning we stop in the living room. I need a minute to re-group and a few sips of coffee. I comb mom's hair while she sits on the sofa and she acknowledges this with a subtle, "That feels nice." I always seem to cringe at that statement. I'm not sure why, but I think it has something to do with the normalcy of it all. She can't remember how to sit down, or even who I am most of the time, but somehow she knows to acknowledge the joy of having her hair brushed? This disease is an enigma. Anyway, I decide to play a Shirley Temple DVD which will keep my well-coiffed mother safely occupied while I prepare breakfast.

Breakfast is usually non-eventful. The one thing my mother hasn't lost is her appetite. However, this morning I made the mistake of placing too many different items on her plate and her perceived confusion is having an adverse effect. The only remedy to this dilemma is removing the plate, cutting everything up, mixing it together and placing it back in front of her. Fortunately, that predicted snow has finally arrived and I use the large window, and the dancing flakes, as a diversion at this simplest of tasks. My appetite is lost in the tragedy and it is all I can do to keep her company while she eats.

During this time I always seem to experience flashes of the life I no longer get to experience. Momentary glimpses of **Saigon 39** in Kansas City, turning the corner towards the **Isle of Capri Casino**, or sitting at my favorite slot machine in front of **The House of Blues** at **Mandalay Bay**, sends a shiver up my spine and briefly haunts my heart. For that fleeing moment in time, I am actually there and the weight of my sacrifice warms my soul. I know I will visit all of those places again and I take these abbreviated apparitions as notice that the time to take a break is at hand.

With her breakfast now completed we adjourn to the living room and all the glory that is satellite television. With a plethora of viewing options available, I am sure to find something to engross the mysterious mind of my mother. Usually something involving children could peek her limited interest. This morning there is nothing either of us finds interesting, so I reach into the DVD library and choose, **It's A Wonderful Life**. I didn't watch it during the holidays and mom still seems to have some grasp of the time period and, of course, Jimmy Stewart. This kills a couple of hours and, as Clarence finally gets his wings, it's time to make the first of several bathroom visits. Once again the procedure is frustrating but eventually we complete the mission and it's back to the living room and some hopeful channel surfing.

Throughout each morning I try to guide my mother through something that resembles conversation. I think it is important to exercise whatever cells remain in that brain of hers and from time-to-time the babble that comes out of her mouth is quite entertaining. Today it is all about pretty ladies and children playing in a yard. Somewhere in her brain is a stubborn cell full of fragmented memories of childhood. Her fondness and recollection of children is amazing. They are always happy and, the little boys are always trying to get something by the little girls. Just like the real world. The pretty lady part puzzles me, but I believe it has more to do with kindness than physical appearance. In any event, it is great to see her so animated and I enjoy guiding her through these conversations.

As our discussion begins to wane, I hear the lunch bell clanging in the distance and I know naptime is just a short time away. Lunch is usually a simple affair and today was no exception. With the mounting snow outside I felt that a grilled cheese sandwich and some hot tomato soup would be appropriate. It's quick, easy and always a winner as far as mom is concerned. She no longer dips her sandwich in the soup but she does consume it all and, when asked if it was okay, replies with a smile, "Delicious."

One more stop at the bathroom and then it's naptime for mom. She almost instantly falls asleep and, as I attach the gate at the top of the stairs, I smile, thank God and breathe free air, if only for an hour or so. I clean up the kitchen, toss in a load of laundry and sit down at the computer to begin writing what you've been reading. It's sort of surreal when you think about it. Anyway, I get this chapter started, hit a wall and decide to just take some 'me' time and vegetate in front of the television. Peace comes in many shapes and sizes.

With naptime over, it's time for Rachel, Giada and all my new friends on the Food Network. Thank God for our absurd obsession with food. Not only do I get to expand my culinary skills, but also mom seems to lock into the kitchen settings and beautiful women who occupy them. She stares, smiles and is somehow transformed by the familiarity of it all. Occasionally, when Giada starts waxing Italian, mom really seems to perk up and take notice. She's always had an affinity for the Italian heritage that came to her by marriage. Can you blame her? I usually take the time between Giada and Rachel to converse with mom. With thoughts of 'Italiano' still lurking in her head, I ask about her husband and in-laws, and, of course, food. I really have to guide her through this and I'm not sure if she is talking or just returning my volley. However, it seems like a real conversation. When she smiles, and gets animated by the subject, I know that I have achieved my goal.

As dinnertime approaches, and the caregiving clock continues to tick away at another day, two thoughts always enter my mind. The first thought is almost a constant, "I can't believe I'm still doing this!" I am always amazed at the perseverance and infinite amount of love and patience I obviously possess for this woman sitting at the dining room table. Who'd thought I would still be here keeping all well within her darkening world? The second thought is, "I can't believe I'm still doing this!" Fortunately, the good always seems to outweigh the bad and what I can't seem to believe becomes quite believable. After all, I have placed myself in a position to actually affect the life of someone I love. It would be a good guess to say at least half of my siblings would argue that point, but the truth is that if she had been placed in a nursing home those many years ago, it is very likely my mother would have left this earth in a state of confusion. It's funny, but as absurd as that is, I still find a way to let their apathy affect me. Most of the time I can just let it go, convincing myself that their opinion doesn't really matter. And besides, these are the same siblings who still believe that George Bush is a good president! My heart knows the worth of my quest and, somewhere in that mind of hers, my mother knows too.

I could fictionalize the dinner menu with some culinary extravaganza, but, to keep it real, I will say we had one of my mother's favorite meals...Polish sausage, sauerkraut, mashed potatoes and Jewish rye bread with butter. Not a fancy meal but very manageable and flavors my mother still seems to enjoy. This was the meal we were treated to as children and one I often made when I wanted to be reminded of the past. In any event, dinner went off with a unique sense of normalcy that isn't always the norm and, as the day drew to a close, I felt confident I could mark this one off as a success.

As mom scraped a fork across a barren plate and attempted to drink from an empty glass, the time to retire to the living room was at hand. This small idiosyncrasy is a reality check for me.

The post dinner world was normal, abnormal and magical...all at the same time. Gathering around the television after dinner is almost an American tradition and we were big on tradition. Prompting conversation or reaction to the nightly news was an interesting exercise and on occasion would inspire an animated discussion that rarely had anything to do with the events of the day. As time passed, and the disease dug it's heals in, any form of communication or conversation is indeed magical. After a few hours of television, mom would rapidly fade into that pre-slumber mode we all experience. Head bobbing and eyes fighting to bear the weight of the sandman's potion, it was finally bedtime. Early on I just escorted mom to the bathroom and ultimately the comfort of her bed. Towards the end, I carried her frail body up those twelve steps, prepped her and gently tucked her in for another silent night. This was my final lap of the day. After cleaning off the dinner table and prepping my coffee pot for the morning brew, I found the way to my bedroom, grabbed the remote, thanked God for another successful day and fell hard into the minor moments of freedom I had before the grind began again.

REVERSAL OF MISFORTUNE

As the fall of our fourth year together started to cloak the summer sun, time's decline began to mimic the plunge of my mother's condition. It had been eight months since the T.I.A. episode and although she did have a brief respite from her disorder, all was back to normal with the audacious advancement of her Alzheimer's disease. The confusion returned full throttle, along with the daily disintegration of her motor skills, and the silent nature of our day-to-day existence. It seemed the final stage of our journey had finally begun...or had it?

Within the course of eight days, mom suffered two more T.I.A.s. The first took place as we were getting ready for yet another day. Never again do I want to witness anything that horrendous. A few uncontrollable spasms, accompanied by an inane stare told me that trouble was nearby. As we cautiously made our way from the bathroom back to her bed, it hit hard and the look on her face, and the moan of pain that she released, sent ice through my veins. I cradled her frozen body as it slowly dropped to the floor. Quickly, the chaos subsided and, as the eerie wheezing began, I recognized this monster and knew this would either subside or go the route that would probably lead to the end of our situation. So we sat there on the floor and I did all I was capable of doing. I told mom I loved her and stroked her thinning hair.

After just a few long minutes, she returned to an exhausted form of normal. I coaxed her to a sitting position and, with caution lifted her off the floor and placed her in bed. Eventually I got her tucked in and asked if she was hungry; more so for a response than anything else. Of course, she was and it was breakfast in bed for mom. The rest of the day consisted of continuous pampering, praying and patrolling my mother's condition. The following morning I entered my mom's room with a lot of apprehension only to find a very healthy and animated woman sitting there.

Each morning following that episode I approached my mother's room with caution and apprehension. Squinted eyes and attentive ears ran point on every ascent I made to begin our day. On the eighth day my scout signaled trouble ahead and I quickly did a mental re-group and advanced towards the looming adversity. Another T.I.A. had assumed my mother's position and, after successfully defeating this follow-up assault, I knew I needed help in developing a plan of prevention for the future or surely there would be none.

Apathetic speculation was the best that anyone could offer. Perhaps Diabetes was the culprit? Maybe it is a mild form of Epilepsy? No one seemed to have an answer for me so I took it upon myself to solve the mystery. Since the T.I.A. is a temporary restriction of blood flow, I added aspirin to mother's diet to thin the blood and, perhaps, aid in that flow. She took two children's aspirin with breakfast and two more each night with dinner. I'm no expert on Diabetes but I do know that diet and orange juice are important in combating it, so I tweaked our already healthy menu and served O.J. with each meal. I also added more prayer to my daily routine albeit with a diminishing amount of faith. Finally, I summoned all of the love I possessed and bestowed it upon the woman who always did the best she could for me.

And then the most curious thing occurred. Mom started getting better. Perhaps I should qualify that statement. Of course she still had, and always would have, Alzheimer's disease. She still had a hard time knowing who I was or where she was and even the names of her children. However, she did begin to become much more animated. No longer did she just sit and stare, occupying space and struggling for a simple response to life. Now we indulged in conceptual conversations that, albeit waver near the surreal, were refreshing and seemed to possess rejuvenating powers. Here is a sample of her side of one of our conversations: "They didn't want Walter...my brother and sister, I showed them sweetness. Start...somebody else has started it out and I love them and the tiny babies...I think that Walter...it's always that way...one of the words is ...Walther...Hey Jay, why don't you just lay your head up, forever and ever, amen. Walter knows him and I told her that while was together sending the house to town and they come out with their hands in the head scratching and smelling...yea, that was Walter, yea...I'm just riding...because I need love...because it was Walter...just standing there, yea, stay out their hoping Walther Orsech, I said Walter and Steven, because I, his name was Walter..."

We danced with purposeful understanding accompanied by sly smiles that let me to know someone is still occupying her mind. Kisses on the cheek and forehead were almost always acknowledged with an adorably bashful, "Oh, I got a kiss!"

There will be days when the camouflage is revealed and the strength of the disease reminds you that all is not right with the world. Shallow stares will replace smiles. Bewilderment will once again rule the day. On these days I can literally see my mother fade into the shadow of the disease. If you are fortunate enough to experience a brief reversal of the misfortune of Alzheimer's, beware of this revelation. It is far too easy to become accustom to this new behavioral charade. Confusion will scramble reason and you will fall into a false sense of security. The norm will become slanted towards a mirage that must be appreciated, but not believed.

For example: this morning mom woke up very energetic, with a smile on her face and a childlike animation as we spoke of tomorrow's Easter celebration. Her time in the shower was very cooperative and it was an enchanting experience as we eased into the start of the day. Then I sat her at the dining room table, turned my back for just a moment and bam, the woman with Alzheimer's disease had returned. She spent the better part of the morning in that funk but after a trip to the bathroom and a short nap, the funk returned to wherever it resides and my animated mother reappeared.

Early on in the campaign, mom was doing her best to fight off the inevitable, but would frequently succumb to the grasp of Alzheimer's. Eventually, the disease all but conquered her resolve and totally possessed her spirit. That's what makes this new manifestation so phenomenal. No one has an explanation. The doctors can simply say that this isn't supposed to happen. Dr. Flaherty feels that this reversal is related to the exceptional care I give my mother. Perhaps that is true. Perhaps love is the ultimate answer.

"See me, feel me, touch me, heal me!" These words by Pete Townsend ring very true when it comes to dealing with Alzheimer's disease. I have always given my mother a great deal of human touch over the years. After the T.I.A. episodes I added much more touch and feel to our daily routine. Perhaps the aspirin has helped postpone the plaque build-up? Or, perhaps the power of human touch really can conquer all and love may just be our greatest healer.

P.S. I LOVE YOU

On too many occasions I have heard the family members and friends of Alzheimer's victims say, "That's not my mother sitting there." Or, "I want to remember my father as he was." If I squint my eyes hard enough I could almost see the logic in those observations. However, I like to look to at things with my eyes wide open and what I saw is a loved one lost in the midst of a nightmare. I saw a woman who needed my love and attention, now more than ever before. I saw someone who gave the best she was capable of, sacrificing unknown adventures for the love of her family. And though she was barely treading the waters of reality, I still saw my mother.

Towards the end, I couldn't help but feel regret for all the words that were never shared. Edward Young said that, "Procrastination is the thief of time." I never really knew how accurate that observation was until I took on the caregiver roll. Too many words that should have been said were now lost. Time had erased any chance that those sentiments would adhere to the mind or heart of my mother. We still shared, *I love you's*, but I know now that my mother's response was mostly mechanical. She no longer had any sense of reality to guide her. However, I'd like to believe that, from time to time, her emotions found their way through the fog, long enough to see that someone really was there for her.

My father died a few weeks before I graduated from high school. Our last words were angry ones and time never gave me a chance to repair that. Now there isn't a day that goes by that I don't regret the words and abhor the curse that procrastination has left me with.

Perhaps taking care of my mother, in some small way, helped me mend that cosmic fence.

The point here is simple. When dealing with Alzheimer's, or any fatal disease for that matter, time is not on your side. Sometimes putting things off until tomorrow will be thwarted by the possibility that tomorrow might be too late. Find the words, seek the sentiment and share it. Do not think that tomorrow will be a better day because as I have found out, procrastination really is a thief and the only way to avoid it's consequence is to always do today what may be too late to do tomorrow.

THE END

All you need is love, five little words that define the motivation that must be present for us to do what it is we do. However, as much as I love the opportunity to quote Lennon and McCartney, in caregiving, there must also be much, much more. Hopefully you've just read this book and if so, you understand that running neck-and-neck with love is patience. I don't care how much you love a person, if you're short on tolerance and understanding, your mission will be a failed one. The good news is that love can actually boost your level of patience. It can act like a steroid that enhances your ability to sustain order and tolerate the most absurd of situations. When this journey began, my patience, or famous lack thereof, was a big concern for me. Would I be able to withstand that primal urge to fly off the handle as the frustration of Alzheimer's began to dig beneath my skin? At first it was a struggle to govern the baffling aspects of the disease. Eventually it sunk in that this confused and unpredictable woman truly was unable to maintain any discipline and that sole, sad realization somehow helped ease the fervor. There were many days when counting to ten helped bridge the space between tranquility and detonation. Even at the end of 11-years and 24-hours-a-day exposure, this disease continues to frustrate and fascinate me.

Patience must also be present with family members, friends and, for that matter, society as a whole. As caregivers, our sole responsibility, in most cases, is our loved one. We rely on others, specifically family members, for moments of freedom and tidbits of normalcy in the midst of chaos. When that taste of reality is abated by apathy, it is easy to become angry and just a little paranoid. In my case, I have learned to accept it. Perhaps I naively rationalize the apparent lack of concern of some of my siblings by telling myself they're scared, or the misery is just too much for them to deal with. In the beginning it made me mad as hell, but, in time, I realized you can't force people to care and I relied on my new found patience to accept their absence and appreciate whatever time we share together. Any time you truly love, you must realize with that commitment comes sorrow and pain; it's inevitable. Nothing will alter the love I have for those siblings, however, their apparent lack of interest in our mother's condition or my well-being for that matter, boggles the mind and exercises my newly honed patience.

As Alzheimer's continues its barrage on the masses, more and more people are being made aware of the madness the disease entails. However, there are still many members of society who have no concept of the disorder. Patience is key with these people for their reactions, in many cases, can be frustrating and hurtful. They will look at you as if you are controlling and condescending. They will look upon your loved one as crazy and meddlesome. There was a time when I considered having shirts and jackets made for my mom to wear to advertise her illness in an attempt to ease the ambiguous attitude of onlookers. It would say: *If I seem confused, please be patient. If I seem irritated, please be kind. If I seem happy, please thank God for I have Alzheimer's.* But, with the state of our world today, advertising weakness to society's demons seemed irresponsible. As time's gone by, the world has shrunk for my mother and me. The adventures that defined our first years together are now limited to occasional trips to the home of friends or the parish church. As mom's disease progresses, I find it is becoming increasingly more difficult for everyone concerned to try and keep her active amongst the bustle of society. Daily walks around the neighborhood, and the occasional interaction with neighbors, is the extent of our outside activity.

The love that motivated me to continue this quest metamorphosis into an indefinable emotion that, even in the face of Alzheimer's, bordered on biblical. I found that looking at my mother through eyes that no longer feared the mystery of her fate, was inspirational. As I continue to confront the inevitability of this disease - jumbled speech, botched attempts at eating and disintegrating bladder control - frightened me. The daily decline of consciousness I witnessed is brutal but these are things I had learned to acknowledge and attempted to ignore. Instead, when I looked at my mother, even towards the end, I saw a happy and somewhat graceful dance partner. I saw a woman who I could manipulate with a simple word or phrase and transform her from a dormant vessel into an animated glimpse of who she once was. I saw the woman who gave me life and I like to think my dedication to her has somehow begun to return the deed.

The inevitability of Alzheimer's is death. At this time there is no cure for what I deem the most horrific disease of our time. So, if you are a caregiver or just beginning your journey as one, know that if you see it through, death definitely awaits and that, my friends, is simply the end of the voyage. I can promise you that your crusade will be full of fruitful, fantastic moments that will make the inevitable end seem adorned.

But getting back to the end of your quest; this may be the most difficult phase of a venture you thought had just concluded. When all the dust of final arrangements clears, and the foreign face of everyday life stares you down, the final anxious aspect of caregiving can completely confound you.

Mornings arrive and purpose seems to require a Rosetta Stone tape to interpret your next move. In the beginning, the dubious state of freedom is always confounded by small voices sounding the alarm to time spent too far away from home. I still experience moments of incredulity as I attempt to re-enter society. Although I never actually left society, the 'real' world has become a very intimidating place.

When your focus is on a loved one, time and trends take a back seat to necessity. So when your caregiving responsibilities cease, you will have a whole lot of catching up to do. Social mores must be reacquired as you step cautiously through the mine fields of civilization. It is helpful to have a guide who can hold your hand and care a little for you.

For example, when I began caregiving gasoline was $0.86 a gallon. When mom passed away it was $1.16. Imagine that the world had never heard of Bill Gates but when you awaken from your years of caregiving you discover his Microsoft company had exceeded $1 Billion in sales. That's how it feels. Kind of like walking through a retro shop.

Another post-caregiving quandary is actually caregiving. It's as if the time spent as a custodian for your loved one is a drug and when the need or supply ends you are faced with pseudo withdrawal symptoms and a desire to care, care, care! And, if you are bold enough, or brave enough, you might try letting someone take care of you for a change.

Unless you are very fortunate, another hurdle in the post-caregiving world will be financial. Not only will you be haunted with the rumination of money not earned while caregiving, you will, in many cases, be struggling to pay off any remaining debt while wandering back into the workforce. This can be extremely difficult and frustrating. But remember, there can be no regret in the caregivers' psyche. The way I handle it is to grin, bear it and check it off as another accomplishment in the string of achievements I accumulated as the caregiver for my mother. That thought alone eases the burden and fizzles out the frustration.

**BEFORE AND AFTER PICTURES OF
MY BEAUTIFUL MOM**

We'll miss you Mom!

VARIOUS NOTES TO ME FROM MOM

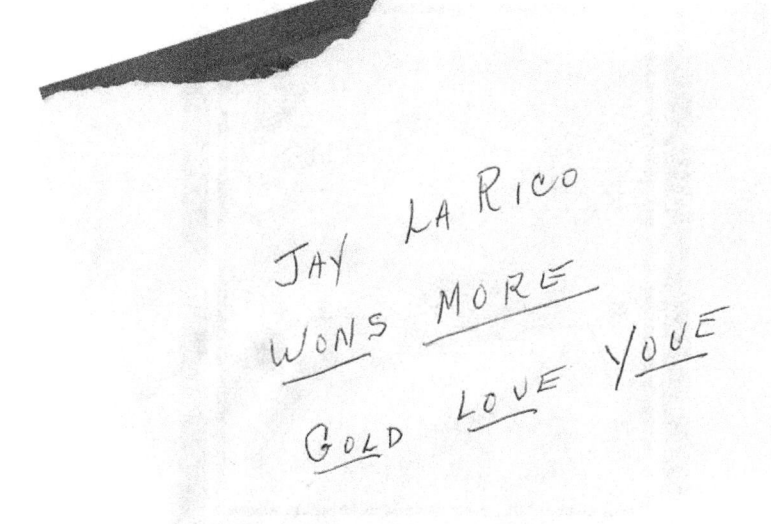

JAY LA RICO
WONS MORE
GOLD LOVE YOUE

GOLD BLESE YOU

ALWESE YOU

MARERE BLESSING
MARY LA RICO

JAY LARICO —

Many good wishes
for a very Merry Christmas
and a Happy New Year.

ABOUT THE AUTHOR

Jay LaRico is a freelance writer and poet who has been writing since he was a child. His short stories and articles have appeared in school newspapers as well as daily publications. In college, Pulitzer Prize-winning poet, Seamus Heaney, praised a small body of his work. Currently working on two novels, Jay's life took a turn when he moved from his home in Kansas City and returned to his native St. Louis to care for his mother who was diagnosed with Alzheimer's disease. From this experience has come this book, **The Choice of Angels.**

Grazie Mille
(Thank you very much)

Betty Hoeffner, my sister, my confidant and my friend. You made this journey a little more bearable.

John LaRico, my brother and mentor, the phone calls saved my life Johnnie Kied, Dee Chavez and every one at Mandalay Bay, Las Vegas. You were my respite destination and salvation.

Beverly and everyone at Bank of America, your tolerance and friendliness with mom will live in my heart forever.

Michelle and everyone at Schnucks® in Florissant, your friendship and appreciation of our situation inspired my European shopping practice.

Mary and George O'Bryan, your friendship and sacrifice made my journey possible.

To my siblings as a whole, the culmination of our lives together was the inspiration for my dedication.

To everyone at Manor Care and Christian Northeast Adult Day Care, your love and dedication to my mother and all others facing her situation was no less than a gift from God.

And finally, to Dr. Joseph H. Flaherty, your wit and wisdom fueled my tenacity.

To schedule Jay LaRico for a book signing,
or speaker at your next event,
email TheChoiceOfAngels@gmail.com

Share your thoughts and experiences with Jay on
The Choice Of Angels Facebook page:
#TheChoiceOfAngels

Visit our website @
http://thechoiceofangels.com/

Made in the USA
Middletown, DE
21 November 2021